Manual of Combined Movements

For Churchill Livingstone:

Publisher: Mary Law
Editorial Co-ordination: Editorial Resources Unit
 Copy Editor: Andrew Gardiner
 Indexer: Laurence Errington
Production Controller: Nancy Henry
Design: Design Resources Unit
Sales Promotion Executive: Hilary Brown

Manual of Combined Movements

Their Use in the Examination and Treatment of Mechanical Vertebral Column Disorders

Brian C. Edwards

BSc BAppSci MPAA FACP

Specialist Manipulative Physiotherapist
Honorary Fellow, Curtin University of Technology
Perth, Western Australia

Churchill Livingstone

EDINBURGH LONDON MADRID MELBOURNE NEW YORK AND TOKYO 1992

CHURCHILL LIVINGSTONE
Medical Division of Longman Group UK Limited

Distributed in the United States of America by Churchill
Livingstone Inc., 650 Avenue of the Americas, New York,
N.Y. 10011, and by associated companies, branches and
representatives throughout the world.

© Longman Group UK Limited 1992

All rights reserved. No part of this publication may be
reproduced, stored in a retrieval system, or transmitted in
any form or by any means, electronic, mechanical,
photocopying, recording or otherwise, without either the
prior written permission of the publishers (Churchill
Livingstone, Robert Stevenson House, 1–3 Baxter's Place,
Leith Walk, Edinburgh EH1 3AF), or a licence permitting
restricted copying in the United Kingdom issued by the
Copyright Licensing Agency Ltd, 90 Tottenham Court Road,
London W1P 9HE.

First published 1992
  Reprinted 1993

ISBN 0-443-04666-2

British Library Cataloguing in Publication Data
A catalogue record for this book is available from the British
Library.

Library of Congress Cataloging in Publication Data
Edwards. B. C. (Brian C.)
   Manual of combined movements: their use in the
examination and treatment of mechanical vertebral column
disorders/Brian C. Edwards.
      p. cm.
   Includes index.
   ISBN 0-443-04666-2
   1. Spine—Examination.   2. Spine—Movements.   I. Title.
   [DNLM: 1. Movement.   2. Palpation.   3. Spinal
Diseases—diagnosis.   4. Spine——physiopathology.
WE 725 E26m]
RD768.E39   1992
617.3'75075–dc20
DNLM/DLC
for Library of Congress

The
publisher's
policy is to use
**paper manufactured
from sustainable forests**

Produced by Longman Singapore Publishers (Pte) Ltd.
Printed in Singapore

Preface

The purpose of this manual is simply to draw attention to the use of combined movements when examining and treating mechanical disorders of the vertebral column. It is intended that the manual be used in conjunction with the more complete texts of Maitland (1986) and Grieve (1988).

Although the use of combined movements is not always necessary — adequate results being obtained by standard examination procedures — there are times when they are helpful. Often, with the more difficult mechanical problems, their use is essential.

The principles of technique selection in relation to movement pattern and category of patient (i.e. acute, subacute and chronic) have been suggested with the intention of providing a basis for the choice of initial direction. The rationale has then been expanded to incorporate a progression of treatment related to direction of movement and position of joint, rather than grade of movement; however, an understanding of the principles of the graded movement is essential to the total concept.

Generally, it is hoped that the concept and use of combined movements will be seen to be a helpful and simple adjunct to the management of vertebral column disorders of mechanical origin.

Perth, 1992   B.C.E.

Acknowledgements

I would like to thank Mr Chris Barrett MCSP, SRP, Grad.Dip.Manip. Ther.(WA) for his considerable help in collating the material and his useful, constructive comments regarding the text; also Kathy O'Callaghan MAPA, Grad.Dip.Manip.Ther.(WA) for her patience in being such an excellent model for the technique photographs; and finally, my clerical staff, Barbra Livie and Dianne Robinson, whose assistance is greatly appreciated.

B.C.E.

Contents

1.   Subjective examination of the vertebral column

Other authors have written excellent chapters dealing with the subjective examination of patients with spinal complaints (Grieve 1988, Maitland 1986) and the reader is referred to these texts for details of how to carry out a detailed subjective examination. However, there are certain aspects of the subjective examination that are worth emphasizing and these relate specifically to the use of combined movements in the examination and treatment of spinal disorders.

RECORDING SYMPTOMS USING A BODY CHART

A standard orthopaedic examination of the vertebral column includes an accurate account of the symptoms and their distribution. This can be achieved in a number of ways. A body chart is useful, with the therapist marking the chart according to where the patient indicates areas of pain, paraesthesia and anaesthesia. Care must be taken to explain to the patient that it is important and necessary to describe the symptoms experienced at the time of assessment. If the distribution of symptoms has changed, the change can be superimposed on the same diagram, or a separate diagram may be used. This is an important aspect of the examination since a clear understanding of those symptoms that are currently experienced, as compared to those originally experienced, can have an important bearing on both diagnosis of the condition and selection of the treatment techniques.

SYMPTOM BEHAVIOUR

Once descriptions of the symptoms and their distribution have been established, the patient should be questioned about how symptoms in different areas are related to each other (e.g. Has there been an increase in pain in one area, with a corresponding change in another area? In what sequence did the symptoms originally appear?). Such questioning is often omitted in history taking. However, the answers provided by the patient highlight and implicate the anatomical structures likely to be affected, which may be the cause of the patient's symptoms. They can also help in identifying the level of involvement of referred symptoms when it comes to the objective examination. For example, if it is known than right sided suprascapular pain is related to right lateral arm pain, but on anterior palpation of the cervical spine only the more proximal pain can be reproduced, it is likely that treatment at this level may help both symptomatic areas. This is because the different areas of pain are likely to come from the same structure.

The constancy of a patient's symptoms or the variability in the intensity of pain are also important aspects of the history taking and must be established. Following this, activities that cause any change in symptoms should be noted, i.e.:

a. the ease with which symptoms are aggravated;
b. the activities that cause this aggravation;
c. the relation between the type of activity and the duration and intensity of symptoms produced (sometimes called *irritability*).

These are a useful guide to the amount of physical examination or treatment that may be carried out on the first day.

Activities that aggravate, relieve or do not affect the symptoms need to be carefully described and analysed in relation to the anatomy and biomechanics of the vertebral column, and to the distribution of the patient's symptoms. The simple activity of digging in the garden may be performed quite differently by two patients.

Once aggravating and easing factors have been identified, it is useful to evaluate which particular combined movements are being performed during the activity. This is especially important in the case of a patient with a severe or irritable condition, when it is important to identify a pain easing position. Detailed analysis of the aggravating and easing positions/ activities can streamline the objective assessment.

If sitting, standing or lying positions aggravate or relieve the symptoms, this should be carefully noted. Particular attention should be paid to the positions adopted by the patient at the time of examination and treatment.

24-Hour variation

Further questioning elicits the diurnal variation of the patient's symptoms. Significant points may come to notice here and may alert the therapist's suspicions regarding underlying pathologies. For example, prolonged morning stiffness may be a symptom of some inflammatory conditions; significant pain at night may indicate the presence of a serious pathology.

History

The history of present and past attacks of spinal pain, in terms of the type of activity responsible (if any) and the mode of onset of the symptoms, needs to be described clearly by the patient and noted by the physical therapist. The onset of the symptoms is frequently related to and may have resulted from a particular incident or activity. However, it is not unusual for patients to have difficulty remembering the particular incident, as they may regard it as trivial or it may have occurred some time before the onset of the symptoms.

REFERENCES

Grieve G P 1988 Common vertebral joint problems, 2nd edn. Churchill Livingstone, Edinburgh, p 303–307
Maitland G D 1986 Vertebral manipulation, 5th edn. Butterworths, London, p 43–57

2.

Objective examination of the vertebral column

GENERAL CONSIDERATIONS

The term *objective examination* is something of a misnomer. Objectivity in its pure form is difficult to achieve when the physical therapist includes in such examination not only movements but also the patient's description of the symptoms reproduced by the movements.

The objective examination therefore contains some elements that are subjective, in the sense that patient response requires interpretation by the therapist. It is important that constant reference is made to the specific areas of pain for which the patient has come seeking treatment. It cannot be overemphasized that attention to (a) small details of a patient's answers, and (b) individual movements, is essential if the objective examination is to help identify particular structures as likely sources of the patient's symptoms.

The principal aim of the objective examination is to establish the effect of movement of the spine on those symptoms that have already been described by the patient. In doing this, the identification of the muscles, joints and ligaments involved in the patient's disorder is of primary importance. Careful observation is made of the way in which the vertebral column moves: areas of hyper- and hypomobility, and areas of relative muscle hypertrophy or atrophy are assessed.

OBSERVATION

The first part of the examination consists of observation. Three important aspects of observation are: general movement, posture and shape of joints, and gait.

General movement

Observation of the care with which the patient moves while adopting the sitting position or while moving out of such a position, of how the patient moves while disrobing, with any changes in facial expression, assists in the interpretation of the patient's symptoms. A pertinent question to be asked when a particular posture produces pain is, 'Is it *the* pain or is it different from the pain for which you are seeking treatment?' Such observations may suggest to the therapist the movements that are likely to reproduce the symptoms.

Posture and shape of joints

Alterations in posture and joint outline may be of recent or long standing duration, and indeed many so-called postural deformities may well be perfectly normal for a particular individual. It should be emphasized that some fairly obvious deformities, e.g. marked kyphosis, lordosis or scoliosis, may be of no significance in relation to the patient's current symptoms.

SPECIFIC MOVEMENT AND OBSERVATION

At this time, it is important to compare those symptoms and signs produced on movement to those answers given to the related subjective questions. Thus, any links may be established between the symptoms described by the patient and those elicited by the movement.

The distribution of symptoms and the range of movement need to be recorded very carefully. In one patient, buttock pain may be produced during the first 10 degrees of flexion, but the patient may also be able to continue to full range without any alteration in the distribution of the pain. In another patient, buttock pain may also be produced in the first 10 degrees of flexion, but on continuing the movement toward full range the pain may progress to the calf. *Both patients have the same range of forward flexion but they produce quite different symptoms, which need to be treated quite differently.* Similar situations occur in the cervical spine.

The effect of a controlled amount of overpressure (i.e. gentle passive forcing of the movement from the patient's end range further into range) is also necessary under certain circumstances, not only to observe the way the symptoms react, but also to test the *end feel* of the physiologic movement. The end feel of a movement is the relationship between the pain experienced and the resistance to movement. Such resistance may be due to intrinsic muscle spasm or tightness of the ligaments and capsule of the joint.

The end feel of the physiologic movement may be different to the end feel with localized passive movement procedures. However, quite distinct solid, springy, soft or hard end feelings may be distinguished. The end feel needs to be noted because if there is a difference between what is found with localized procedures compared to the more general movement procedures, then an attempt needs to be made to find those differences and the possible reasons for them.

The return from the flexed to the upright position is also an important movement to monitor, both in terms of the way the vertebral column moves and the production of symptoms. This applies in both the lumbar and cervical spine. A postural scoliosis or tilt may be seen on adoption of the erect position, but this may not be evident on bending forward. Another important aspect of assessment of flexion and the return to the upright position is the reproduction of a painful arc, i.e. pain that is produced through a part of the range and then is eased as the movement continues. This can happen either during the flexion movement or during the return to the upright position. The range within which such symptoms are produced, as well as the distribution of the symptoms, should be recorded carefully and related, if possible, to the subjective findings. Often, those patients with painful arcs are slower to respond to treatment, particularly if the painful arc is variable in its position in the range.

On occasion, symptoms may be produced some time after the movement has been completed (i.e. *latent pain* is seen). This latent pain possibly may have a large inflammatory component in its production or etiology. Occasionally, repeated flexion movements or varying the speed of the movement may be necessary to reproduce this symptom.

General assessment of standard active physiologic movements
In addition to recording the ranges of movements that are available and the way in which the vertebral segments move, detailed attention must also be given to (a) the distribution of the symptoms, and (b) the type of symptoms involved with each movement. The patient's descriptions of these symptoms are highly important. Comparison needs to be made between various activities as elicited during the subjective questioning and those produced and observed in the objective testing. Similar descriptions of type of symptoms, as well as distribution, are important (i.e. the pain may be described as diffuse, lancinating or referred to a limb, etc.).

At this stage, the therapist should look for similarities between movement of general daily activities that bring on the symptoms and the active movements that elicit the pain. For example, a patient may report that bending activity in the garden for about one hour brings on back pain, while on subsequent examination one repetition of forward flexion is reported to produce the same pain. Careful questioning is required to define the type and distribution of the symptoms, as sustained flexion (if that is the movement he adopts while gardening) is unlikely to produce the same quality and quantity of pain as would be produced by one movement of flexion.

In the case of the cervical spine, a patient may report that the cervical pain is only brought on after watching television for, say, five minutes, therefore sustained movements will also need to be examined.

Objective examination of the vertebral column

Table 2.1 Neurological table

Spinal level	Myotome	Reflex	Dermatome	Sclerotome
C1	Rectus capitus anterior			
C2	Rectus capitus posterior major and minor, with obliquus capitus superior		Crown of head, extending down posteriorly as far as the base of the occiput	
C3	Scalene muscles		Posterolateral aspect of head; anterior aspect of neck	
C4	Trapezius and levator scapulae		Shoulder, over trapezius and deltoid	Clavicle
C5	Deltoid	Biceps	Lateral aspect of arm as far as wrist	Medial scapula; lateral aspect of humerus
C6	Biceps	Biceps and brachioradialis	Lateral aspect of arm, extending into medial two digits	Lateral scapula; posterior humerus; lateral aspect of radius; 1st metacarpal
C7	Triceps	Triceps	Posterior arm; anterior forearm, extending into the middle digits	Lateral scapula; medial humerus; proximal and medial aspect of radius, extending over middle digits
C8	Extensor pollicis longus; flexor digitorum profundus		Medial arm, extending into the medial two digits	Distal third of posterior humerus; distal ulna and medial two digits
T1	Palmar and dorsal interosseous		Medial arm as far as wrist	
L2	Iliopsoas		Superior aspect of anterior thigh	Iliac crest; medial upper femur; posterior sacrum
L3	Quadriceps	Quadriceps	Lateral thigh, extending medially to cover the knee	Iliac crest; anteromedial femur; patella
L4	Tibialis anterior	Quadriceps	Lateral thigh, extending across to cover medial tibia as far as the ankle	Ischial tuberosity; ilium; anterior upper half of tibia; neck of femur
L5	Extensor hallucis longus		Posterior aspect of thigh; lateral lower leg; lateral side of dorsum of foot	Greater trochanter; posterior femur; upper half of fibula; medial tibia and anteromedial foot, extending to big toe
L5 (and S1)	Extensor digitorum longus			
L5 and S1	Posterior femoral muscles			
S1	Peroneus longus and brevis	Ankle	Posterior thigh; lateral lower leg; lateral toes and foot	Posterior femur; posterolateral tibia and anterior fibula; extending into foot to middle toes
S2	Flexor digitorum longus		Posteromedial thigh and leg extending to the heel	Lateral foot and lateral toes
L4 and L5 (S1 and S2)	Gluteus maximus			

Such careful questioning can help both in diagnosis as well as in the selection of a treatment technique.

Combined movements

Habitually, movements of the vertebral column occur in combination across planes rather than as pure movements in one plane only. For this reason, the usual objective examination of the lumbar spine should be expanded to incorporate combined movements, because symptoms and signs produced by lateral flexion, flexion, extension and rotation as pure movements may alter when these movements are performed in a combined manner.

The same general principles as described above are incorporated with the combined movement examination of the vertebral column, and the aim is to highlight aspects of the examination findings of the standard examination. The specific principles of the combined movement examination are related to simple biomechanical observations.

3. Lumbar spine

Objective examination of the lumbar spine

Gait

Obvious gait alterations can be observed initially. Changes such as altered weight distribution and lack of mobility in hips, knees or ankles or a positive Trendelenburg sign may be noted. With the exception of the latter, lack of mobility may arise from inhibition of movement due to pain originating in the lumbar spine, or due to a previous unrelated peripheral joint involvement.

SPECIFIC MOVEMENT AND OBSERVATION

The patient needs to be undressed sufficiently to allow observation of the whole of the spine as well as the lower limbs.

Observation from behind

When observing from behind, the following may be observed and variation noted:

1. Altered leg length
2. Altered shoulder height
3. Position of head on neck and neck on shoulders
4. Kyphosis or lordosis (exaggerated or diminished)
5. Position of scapulae
6. Valgus or varus deformity of knees and feet
7. Scoliosis (postural and structural)
8. Position of sacrum and iliac crests
9. Prominence or depression of vertebral spinous processes
10. Skin contour and colour.

Observation from in front

When observing from the front, the clinician should take note of the following features:

1. Height or level of iliac crests

2. Position or level of knees
3. Shape of trunk
4. Relative position of shoulders, head and feet
5. Skin contour.

Observation from the side

When observing from the side, the clinician should be aware of:

1. Position of head
2. Shape of cervical, thoracic and lumbar spinal curves (any increased or decreased kyphosis or lordosis)
3. Skin contour.

Movements

The lumbar spine is most easily examined from behind.

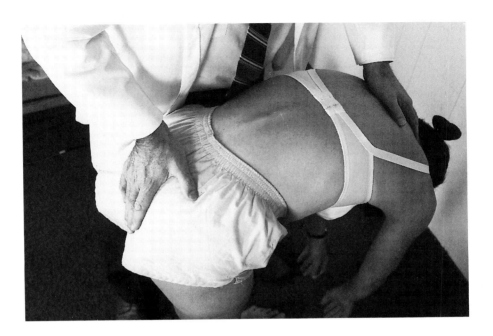

Fig. 3.1   **Examination of flexion of the lumbar spine**

Patient position: Standing.

Therapist position: Standing at the side of the patient.

Hand position: The therapist's right hand is placed over the patient's sacrum; the left hand is placed over the patient's thorax.

Movement: The patient is asked to bend forward to the point where there is any increase in the symptom complex. This flexion range is usually recorded by measuring the distance from the outstretched fingertips to the floor, or in relation to the position of the fingertips on the legs (e.g. patella, midthigh, etc.). The patient is then asked to move in a controlled manner further into the painful range. This range, and any alteration in the symptoms, are noted.

Assessment during flexion

Not only is the full range of movement noted, considerable attention is also paid to the way in which the individual vertebrae move during flexion. Areas of hypo- and hypermobility are recorded as well as any deviation from the median sagittal plane. Surface contour should be carefully considered, particular note being paid to areas of prominence or depression.

On occasion, it is important to hold the full range position of flexion for a period of time. This becomes a necessary part of the examination especially if, during the subjective examination, an activity involving sustained flexion is reported by the patient as a position where symptoms are eased. Such a procedure is valuable because if the symptoms are *not* eased, more detailed questioning and examination is necessary.

The return from the flexed to the upright position is also an important movement to monitor, both in terms of the way the vertebral column moves and the production of symptoms. A postural scoliosis or tilt may be seen on adoption of the erect position, which was not evident on bending forward. Another important aspect of assessment of flexion and the return to the upright position is the reproduction of a painful arc, i.e. the pain that is produced through a part of the range and which then eases as the movement continues. This can happen either during the flexion movement or during the return to the upright position. The range within which such symptoms are produced, as well as the distribution of the symptoms, should be recorded carefully and related, if possible, to the subjective findings. Often, those patients with painful arcs respond to treatment more slowly, particularly if the painful arc is variable in its position in the range.

As well as general observation of changes in signs and symptoms on full range flexion, particular consideration needs to be given to the way in which motion segments are moving.

On flexion, there is a cephalad movement of the inferior zygapophyseal facets at one level in relation to the superior facets of the level below. This is accompanied by stretching of the soft tissues of the posterior elements of the motion segment, including the posterior parts of the disc and the canal structures, as well as the posterior ligaments, capsules and muscles. There is accompanying compression of the anterior parts of the disc (nucleus and anterior annulus, including the anterior longitudinal ligament).

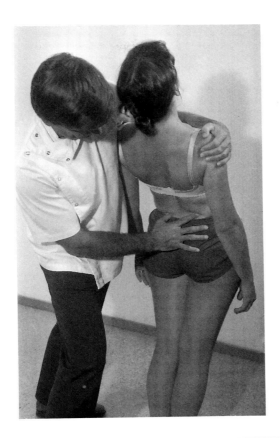

Fig. 3.2	**Examination of extension of the lumbar spine**

Patient position: Standing.

Therapist position: Standing behind the patient.

Hand position: The therapist's left arm is placed around the anterior aspect of the patient's upper chest to take hold of the patient's opposite shoulder. The right hand is placed over the patient's sacrum.

Movement: Extension of the lumbar spine.

Measurement can be made of the distance the finger tips pass down the posterior aspect of the thigh. Areas of hypo- and hypermobility are observed, as well as the distribution of symptoms at the end of range and through the range. Overpressure, repeated and sustained movement are used as necessary.

Lumbar spine

The effect of extension on the motion segment is such that there is caudal movement of the inferior zygapophyseal facet of a vertebra on the facets of the vertebra below. There is also a compression of the posterior parts and stretching of the anterior parts of the intervertebral disc.

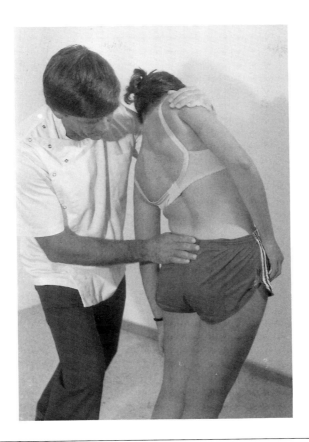

Fig. 3.3   **Examination of left lateral flexion of the lumbar spine**

Patient position: Standing.

Therapist position: Standing behind and to the left of the patient.

Hand Position: The therapist's left arm is placed around the anterior aspect of the patient's upper chest to take hold of the right shoulder. The right hand is placed over the sacrum with the thumb extending over the left iliac crest.

Movement: Lateral flexion to the left.

Areas of hypo- and hypermobility can be observed at segmental levels by closely matching the movement behaviour of the vertebrae, comparing the relative movement of the motion segment(s) with those above and below, and their sideways movement behaviour compared one to the other. As with flexion, the use of overpressure, repeated and sustained movements may be necessary, in addition to the observance of deformity and presence or absence of a painful arc.

It can be seen that on lateral flexion to the left, examining the left zygapophyseal joints, there is a caudad sliding of the inferior facet of the joint on the superior facet of the vertebra below, and structures associated with the left side of the motion segment are thus compressed. In the same movement of left lateral flexion, looking at the right zygapophyseal joints, there is a cephalad sliding of the inferior facet on the superior facet of the vertebra below. This stretches structures on the right side of the motion segment.

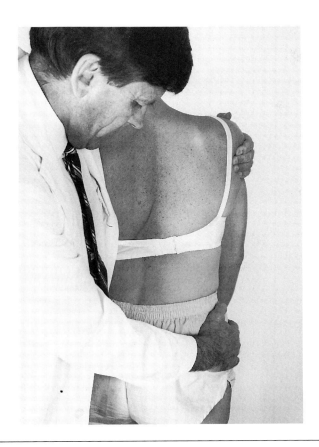

Fig. 3.4   **Examination of left axial rotation**

Patient position: Standing.

Therapist position: Standing on the patient's left side.

Hand position: The therapist's left arm is placed around the anterior aspect of the patient's trunk, to take hold of the patient's right shoulder. The right hand takes hold of the patient's right ilium.

Movement: The pelvis is rotated to the right while applying counter resistance to the patient's upper trunk.

Rotation as a testing procedure is not a movement that often produces significant alteration in signs and symptoms. Strangely enough, it is usually preferred as a passive movement treatment technique by therapists.

Examination of combined movements of the lumbar spine

MECHANICAL PRINCIPLES

In the lumbar spine, the basic principle is to combine movements that have similar mechanical effects on the motion segment, and to observe if symptoms are increased or decreased by such manoeuvres. On flexion, there is a cephalad movement of the inferior zygapophyseal facet of, for instance, L4, on the superior zygapophyseal facet of L5. The posterior elements, i.e. the posterior part of the intervertebral disc, the posterior longitudinal ligament, the ligamentum flavum and the capsules of the zygapophyseal joints are all stretched. The anterior structures are compressed.

With right lateral flexion, for instance, the left inferior zygapophyseal facet of L4 moves upwards on the left superior zygapophyseal facet of L5. This movement produces a stretching of the elements on the left side of the motion segment, with compression of the right side. When flexion and right lateral flexion are combined, the stretching effects on the left are increased, and decreased on the right.

With extension, there is downward movement of the inferior zygapophyseal facet (e.g. of the L4 vertebra on the superior zygapophyseal facet of L5). This is accompanied by compression of the posterior elements of the motion segment. When the movements of right lateral flexion are combined with extension, there is an increase in the compressive effects on the right and a decrease on the left.

| Fig. 3.5 | **Examination of left lateral flexion in flexion** |

Patient position: Standing.

Therapist position: Standing on the patient's left hand side, so that the therapist's left iliac fossa is in contact with the patient's left hip.

Hand position: The therapist's right hand is placed around the patient's right anterior superior iliac spine. The therapist's left hand is placed over the patient's right shoulder.

Movement: Active assisted movement of forward flexion and then left lateral flexion.

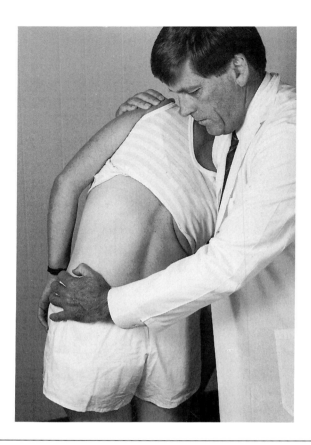

Fig. 3.6   # Examination of flexion in right lateral flexion

Patient position: Standing.

Therapist position: Standing on the patient's right side.

Hand position: The therapist's left hand is placed over the posterior aspect of the patient's left iliac crest. The right hand takes hold of the patient's right shoulder, such that the forearm lies roughly horizontally across the patient's chest at about the level of the suprascapular fossae.

Movement: Active assisted right lateral flexion, and then flexion. Particular effort is made to maintain the position of right lateral flexion while moving the patient into flexion.

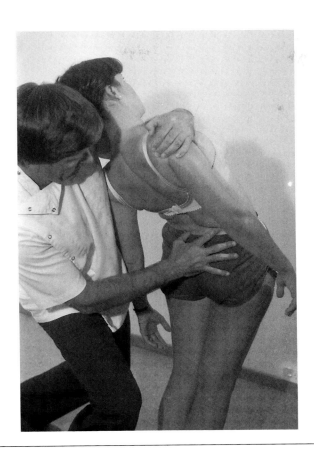

Fig. 3.7   **Examination of left lateral flexion in extension**

Patient position: Standing.

Therapist position: Standing on the patient's left hand side, slightly behind and facing on to the back.

Hand position: The therapist's right hand is placed so that the thumb and the index finger are over the transverse process of the level to be tested. The therapist's left hand is placed anteriorly over the patient's right shoulder.

Movement: Extension and then left lateral flexion.

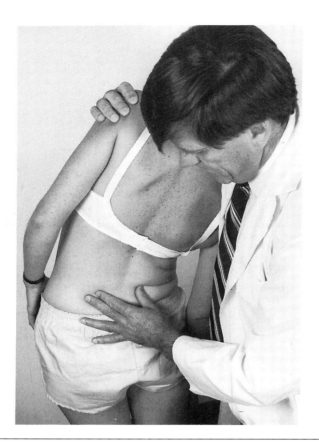

Fig. 3.8   **Examination of extension in right lateral flexion**

Patient position: Standing.

Therapist position: Standing on the patient's right side.

Hand position: The therapist's left hand is placed so that the thumb and the index finger are over the transverse process of the level to be tested. The therapist's right hand is placed anteriorly around the patient's left shoulder.

Movement: The patient is first laterally flexed to the right and then extension is added. Particular effort is made to maintain the right lateral flexion component whilst moving the patient into extension.

Physiological treatment techniques

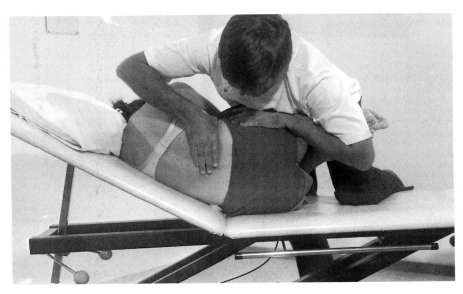

| Fig. 3.9 | **Right lateral flexion in flexion** |

Patient position:	Left side lying in flexion.
Therapist position:	Standing in front of patient with the patient's hips flexed and supported on therapist's left flexed thigh.
Hand position:	The therapist's right hand is placed with fingers over the upper aspect of the spinous process of the vertebrae above. The therapist's left hand is placed over the patient's right iliac crest.
Movement:	Right lateral flexion of the patient's pelvis.

Lumbar spine

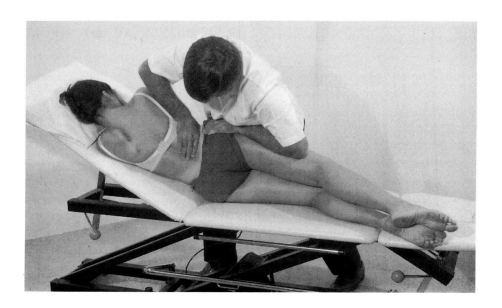

Fig. 3.10   **Right lateral flexion in extension**

Patient position: Right side lying in extension.

Therapist position: Standing in front of the patient.

Hand position: As for right lateral flexion in flexion.

Movement: Right lateral flexion.

Use of accessory movements (confirmation by palpation)

PASSIVE ACCESSORY MOVEMENTS IN COMBINED POSITIONS

The usual accessory movements of transverse, central and unilateral pressure may also be carried out in combined positions. The lumbar spine is placed in the combined positions described above and the appropriate accessory movements are performed. The relevance of examining accessory movements in combined positions of the spine is described later in this manual, and the following descriptions are examples of some of the accessory movements that are available for examination in particular combined positions of the lumbar spine.

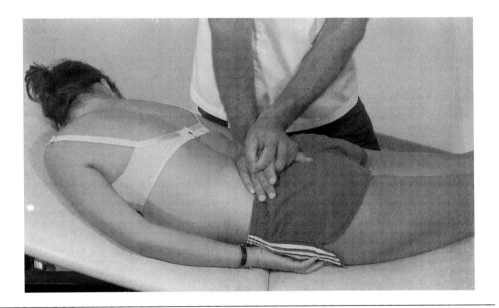

| Fig. 3.11 | **Central vertebral pressure with the lumbar spine in extension and right lateral flexion** |

Patient position: Prone, in extension and right lateral flexion.

Therapist position: Standing on the patient's right hand side.

Hand position: The therapist's right hand is placed so that the area distal to the pisiform is placed over the spinous process of the vertebra to be moved. This hand is reinforced by the left hand gripping the right hand so that the pisiform of

Lumbar spine

the left hand is in line with the anatomical snuff box of the right hand. The left thumb and index finger are placed on the dorsal aspect of the right hand. The middle, ring and little fingers are placed over the palmar aspect of the right hand.

Movement: Posterio-anterior movement.

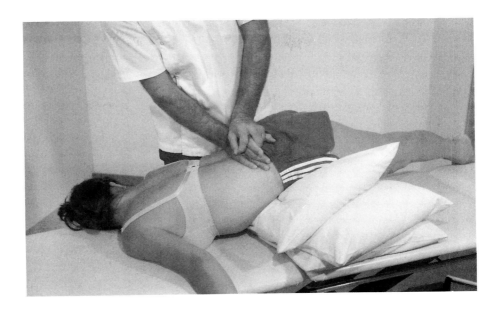

Fig. 3.12   **Central vertebral pressure with the lumbar spine in flexion and right lateral flexion**

Patient position: Prone, with the lumbar spine in flexion and right lateral flexion.

Therapist position: Standing on the patient's right hand side.

Hand position: As for central vertebral pressure in extension.

Movement: Posterio-anterior movement.

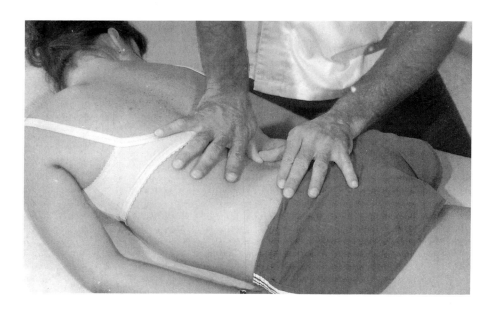

Fig. 3.13   **Transverse pressure to the left with the lumbar spine in extension and right lateral flexion**

Patient position: Prone, with the lumbar spine in extension, and right lateral flexion.

Therapist position: Standing on the patient's right hand side.

Hand position: The therapist's right hand is placed so that the pad of the right thumb is in contact with the spinous process of the vertebra to be moved. The left thumb reinforces this. The fingers of both hands are spread out evenly.

Movement: Transverse pressure to the left.

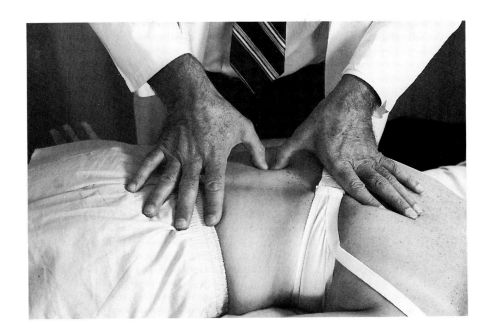

Fig. 3.14

Unilateral pressure on the left with the lumbar spine in flexion and right lateral flexion

Patient position: Prone, in flexion and right lateral flexion.

Therapist position: Standing on the patient's left side, thumbs directed over the facet articulation on the left side.

Movement: Unilateral posterio-anterior pressure.

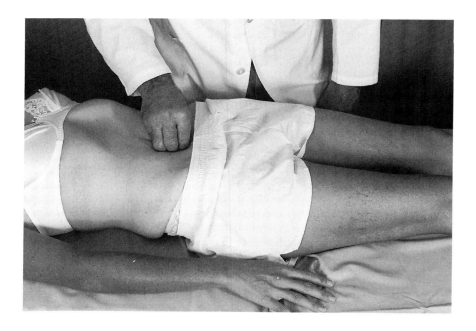

| Fig. 3.15 | **Anterior palpation and mobilization of the lumbar spine** |

Patient position: Supine.

Therapist position: Standing on the patient's left hand side.

Hand position: The fingers of the therapist's right hand are bunched and placed over the patient's abdomen so that palpation is carried out over the palpable anterior part of the lumbar spine.

Movement: Anterior posterior movement.

Passive physiological intervertebral movement (PPIVM) testing

Standard passive physiological tests of the movements of flexion, extension, lateral flexion and axial rotation can also be carried out, and are a useful adjunct to the examination procedures.

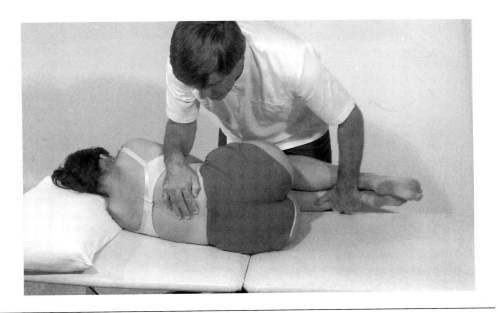

Fig 3.16	**Examination of flexion (PPIVM)**
Patient position:	Left side lying.
Therapist position:	Standing in front of the patient.
Hand position:	The therapist's right hand is placed between the spinous processes of the levels to be tested. The therapist's left hand is placed under the lower legs of the patient.
Movement:	Flexion of the patient's lumbar spine while palpating with the right hand.

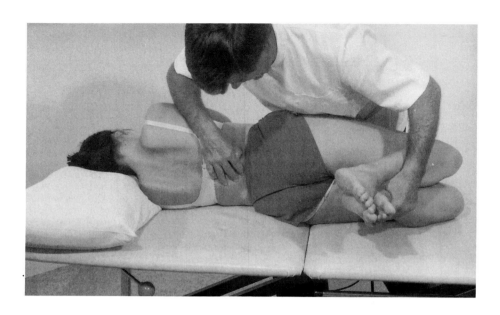

Fig. 3.17   # Examination of extension (PPIVM)

Patient position: As for flexion.

Therapist position: As for flexion.

Hand position: As for flexion.

Movement: Extension of the lumbar spine while palpating between the spinous
                         processes with the right hand.

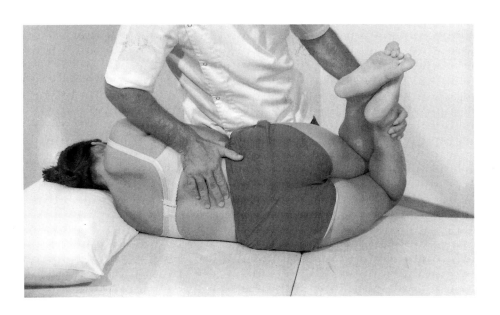

Fig. 3.18   **Examination of right lateral flexion (PPIVM)**

Patient position: As for flexion.

Therapist position: As for flexion.

Hand position: The left hand takes hold of the patient's lower legs by placing them anteriorly around the right ankle. The therapist's right index finger is placed superiorly between the spinous processes of the levels to be tested.

Movement: Right lateral flexion of the lumbar spine.

Lumbar spine

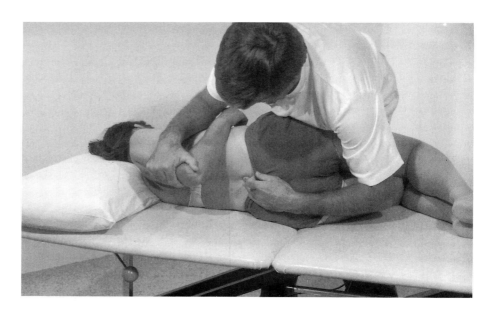

| Fig. 3.19 | **Examination of right rotation (PPIVM)** |

Patient position: As for flexion.

Therapist position: As for flexion.

Hand position: The therapist's left hand is placed so that the left middle finger is placed inferiorly between the spinous processes of the levels to be tested. The therapist's right arm is placed over the patient's right lateral thorax, so that the therapist's right hand takes hold of the patient's distal upper arm.

Movement: Right rotation of thorax.

Sacroiliac joint testing

The following testing procedures may be used to evaluate the range of movement of the sacroiliac joints and to attempt to reproduce the patient's symptoms.

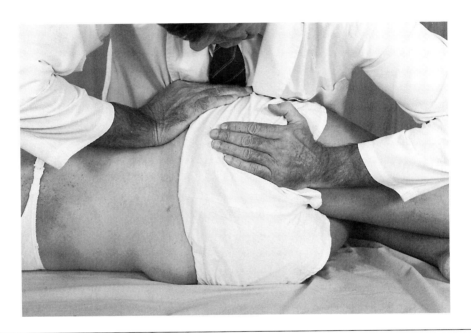

Fig. 3.20	**Sacroiliac joint testing: anterior movement of the right ilium**

Patient position:	Left side lying, with left hip flexed.
Therapist position:	Standing in front of the patient.
Hand position:	The heel of the therapist's right hand is placed over the posterior superior iliac spine; the heel of the therapist's left hand is placed over the ischial tuberosity.
Movement:	Anterior movement of the right ilium.

Lumbar spine

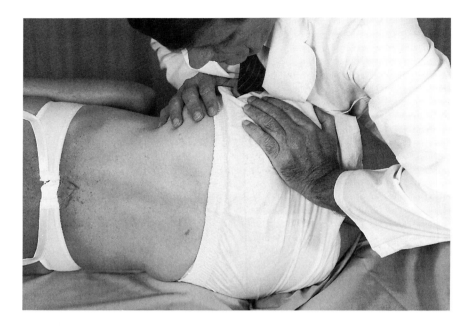

| Fig. 3.21 | **Sacroiliac joint testing: posterior movement of the right ilium** |

Patient position: Left side lying, with left hip flexed.

Therapist position: Standing in front of the patient.

Hand position: The heel of the therapist's right hand is placed over the right anterior superior iliac spine, and the heel of the left hand is placed over the ischial tuberosity.

Movement: Posterior movement of the right ilium.

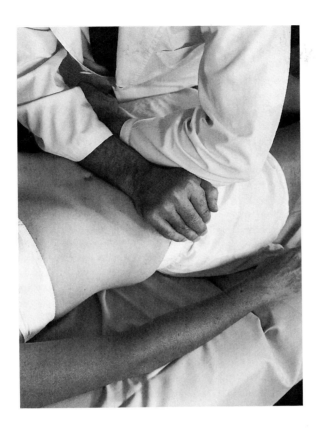

Fig. 3.22   **Sacroiliac joint testing: compression**

Patient position: Supine.

Therapist position: Standing on the patient's left hand side.

Hand position: The heel of the therapist's right hand is placed on the inside of the anterior superior iliac spine; the left hand is placed in a similar position on the left. Forearms are horizontal.

Movement: Lateral movement of both hands.

Lumbar spine

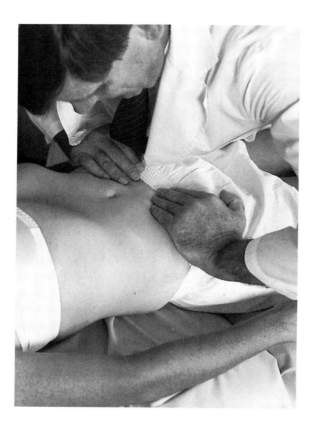

Fig. 3.23   # Sacroiliac joint testing: distraction

Patient position: Supine.

Therapist position: Standing on the patient's left hand side, facing the head.

Hand position: Laterally over the anterior superior iliac spines.

Movement: Medial movement of both hands.

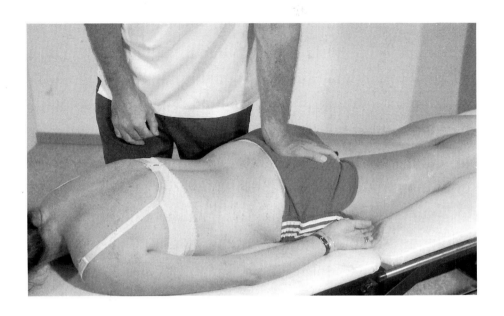

| Fig. 3.24 | **Sacroiliac joint testing: apical pressure of the sacrum** |

Patient position: Lying prone.

Therapist position: Standing to the side of the patient.

Hand position: The left hand is placed over the apex of the sacrum.

Movement: Pressure is directed in a posterio-anterior direction.

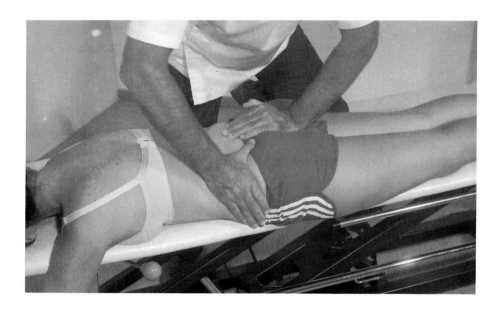

| Fig. 3.25 | **Sacroiliac joint testing: anterior movement of the ilium** |

Patient position: Prone.

Therapist position: Standing on the patient's right side.

Hand position: The therapist's right hand is placed over the crest of the left ilium and the left hand is placed over the apex of the sacrum.

Movement: The right hand moves the left ilium anteriorly; the left hand moves the sacrum cephalad.

Testing for segmental hypermobility

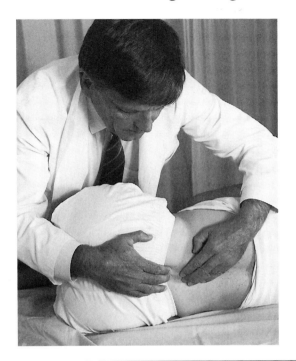 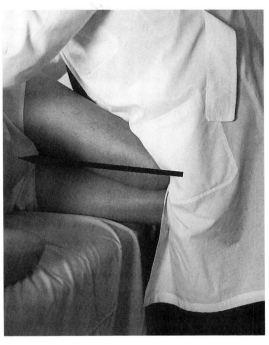

| Fig. 3.26.1 | **Shearing test for detection of hypermobile segments of the lumbar spine (left)** |

| Fig. 3.26.2 | **Shearing test for detection of hypermobile segments of the lumbar spine (showing direction of pressure)(right)** |

Patient position: Lying on the right side.

Therapist position: Standing to the front of the patient, the therapist's upper thighs are placed against the patient's knees.

Hand position: The fingers of the left hand are placed between the spinous processes of the level to be examined.

Movement: Pressure is exerted by the therapist's upper thighs against the patient's knees, along the long axis of the patient's femora, producing a postero-anterior shear between the vertebrae of the level to be examined. Relative movement of the spinous processes is detected with the fingers of the palpating hand.

4. Upper cervical spine

The high cervical spine (occiput — c2) is an area of the vertebral column which does not easily lend itself to physical examination. It is, however, subject to a wide variety of mechanical disorders. The so-called cervical headache has its origin, in many cases, at these levels, as do a number of associated mechanically caused symptoms. The common areas of pain from high cervical mechanical disorders are:

1. sub-occipital and occipital
2. frontal
3. frontal and occipital
4. unilateral, from high cervical to over and in the eye
5. parietal and/or occipital
6. band around the head
7. occipital and crown pain
8. orbit pain (with accompanying watering of the eye)
9. nasal pain

often accompanied by:

a. nausea
b. blurring of vision
c. vertigo
d. enforced rest
e. dulled concentration.

Some of the above symptoms can, of course, be related to conditions other than a cervical headache and would not be suitable for manual therapy techniques, e.g. migraine, vertebral artery syndromes and cranial or cervical tumours. Mechanical disorders of the cervical spine can often mimic these more serious conditions. In cases where true migrainous symptoms are present, manipulation has no part to play. However, many migraine sufferers have a cervical component in the genesis of their symptoms and the severity of migrainous attacks can be lessened after the cervical component has been corrected. Often, signs and symptoms in the high cervical spine are overlooked, due to inadequate examination.

The anatomy of the high cervical spine is unique and, to some degree, more complicated than the rest of the vertebral column. The shapes of the bones and their articulations are distinctly different between the occiput and atlas, atlas and axis, and axis and C3. Such a marked change in anatomy does not occur in such close proximity anywhere else in the vertebral column.

The atlas has no body, but rather an anterior and posterior arch, which join the lateral masses. The superior articular facets are concave and face upwards and medially. The inferior articular surfaces are slightly convex and face downwards and medially. The transverse processes are long.

The axis is quite different in shape. The superior articular facets are slightly convex and laterally inclined. The inferior articular facets are set more posteriorly and are directed downwards and anteriorly to articulate with the third cervical vertebra. Between the superior articular surfaces of the axis, the stout odontoid process projects upwards. At its base posteriorly is a facet for the transverse ligament of the atlas.

Anteriorly, there is a smooth oval facet for articulation with the posterior surface of the anterior arch of the atlas. The transverse ligament passes between the medial tubercles on the lateral masses of the atlas and continues superiorly as the superior longitudinal band to attach to the foramen magnum. Inferiorly, it continues as the inferior band and attaches to the posterior aspect of the body of C2.

From the tip of the odontoid process, the apical ligament passes up to be attached to the foramen magnum, anterior to the superior longitudinal band of the cruciate ligament. The alar ligaments diverge upwards from the sides of the odontoid process to the medial aspects of the occipital condyles.

It is interesting to note that the articulations of the occipito-atlantal and atlanto-axial joints are situated approximately 1 cm anterior to the articulations of the second and third cervical vertebrae.

Although the articular surfaces of the atlanto-occipital and atlanto-axial joints vary somewhat, it is generally agreed that those between the occiput and atlas are concavo-convex, and those between the atlas and axis slightly biconvex (excluding the articulation between the odontoid peg and the anterior arch of the atlas). The main movements which occur between the occiput and atlas are flexion and extension. Because the joint surfaces are concavo-convex, the condyles of the occiput and the articulating surface of the atlas follow the simple concave/convex rule of relative movement.

Although there is some dispute as to whether any rotation occurs between occiput and atlas, passive testing between the mastoid process and transverse process of C1 reveals that a small amount of passive rotation is possible. Lateral flexion of the occiput on the atlas causes the condyles of the occiput to move in the opposite direction to which the head is laterally flexed. There is also some evidence to suggest that lateral flexion is combined with rotation to the opposite side. However, when examining the occipito-atlantal complex with combined movements, the movement of lateral flexion is not as useful as flexion or extension primarily, as it is difficult to increase or decrease the stretch or compression effects of combining lateral flexion with either flexion or extension.

The shape of the articulating surfaces between atlas and axis dictates that the movements which occur are quite different to those occurring between occiput and atlas. Some authors suggest that the occiput and axis should be considered as a segment, rather than the atlas and the axis (Brakman & Penning 1971). This is because of the attachment of the apical superior longitudinal band of the cruciate, the apical ligament from the odontoid tip to the occiput and the alar ligaments from the occiput to the axis. However, while this is a useful concept, any examination of the high cervical spine is not complete without endeavouring to test the individual movements between the occiput and atlas, the atlas and axis.

Physiological movement of the occipito-atlantal complex

FLEXION

On flexion of the head, the condyles of the occiput move dorsally on the superior articulating surfaces of the atlas, tightening the posterior atlanto-occipital membrane.

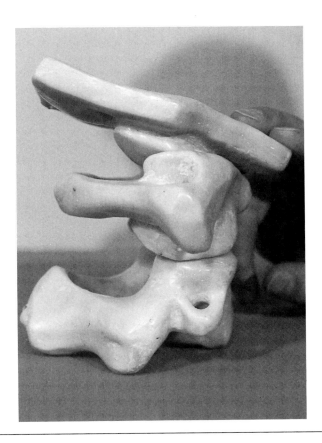

Fig. 4.1   **Flexion of the occipito-atlantal complex**

Upper cervical spine

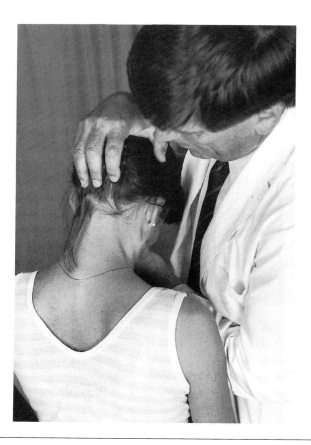

Fig. 4.2   **Method of testing flexion of the occipito-atlantal complex**

Patient position: Sitting.

Therapist position: Standing in the front and to the right of the patient.

Hand position: The therapist's left elbow is flexed and the left forearm is supinated. The left hand cups the symphysis menti. The right forearm is placed over the crown of the head and the fingers of the right hand grip the head below the occiput, but above the arch at C1.

Movement: The head is flexed on the neck, using the left hand to keep the patient's head flexed.

EXTENSION

On extension, the condyles of the occiput move ventrally on the superior articular surface of the atlas and in doing so, tighten the anterior atlanto-occipital membrane and the apical ligament.

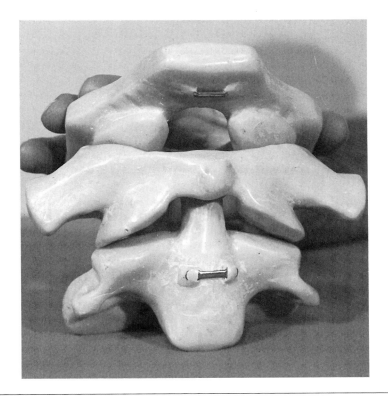

Fig. 4.3   **Extension of the occipito-atlantal complex**

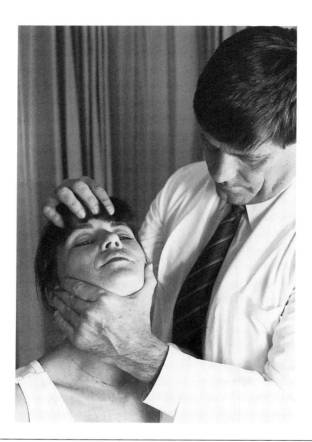

Fig. 4.4   **Method of testing extension of the occipito-atlantal complex**

Patient position: Sitting.

Therapist position: As for flexion.

Hand position: The web of the therapist's left hand is placed under the patient's chin. The right hand is placed over the crown of the head with the fingers extending over the forehead.

Movement: Upper cervical extension, encouraging protrusion of the head with the left hand.

ROTATION

On left rotation of the occiput on the atlas, there is backward movement of the left occipital condyle on the left superior articular surface of the atlas. On the other side, there is forward movement of the right occipital condyle on the right superior condyle of the atlas.

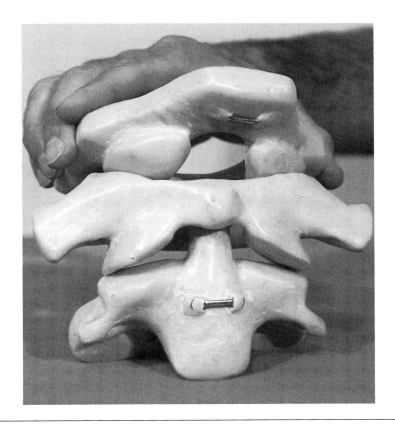

Fig. 4.5   **Left rotation of the occipito-atlantal complex**

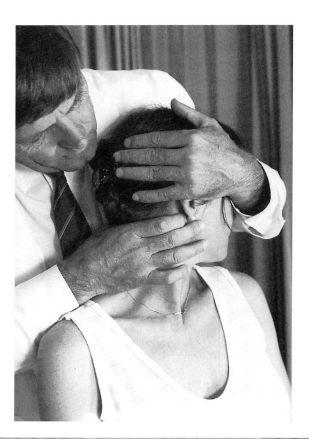

Fig. 4.6

Method of testing left rotation of the occipito-atlantal complex

Patient position: Sitting.

Therapist position: Standing behind patient.

Hand position: Therapist's left hand is placed around patient's head so that the palm of the left hand covers the left temple. The right index finger is placed between the right transverse process of C1 and the right mastoid process.

Movement: The therapist's left arm rotates the patient's head to the left and the movement between the right transverse process of C1 and the mastoid process is assessed.

Physiological movements of the atlanto-axial complex
FLEXION

On flexion, the distance between the posterior arch of the atlas and the spinous process of the axis increases, and there is a gapping of the articular surfaces posteriorly.

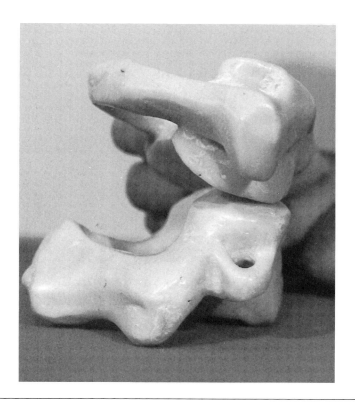

Fig. 4.7   **Flexion of the atlanto-axial complex**

Upper cervical spine

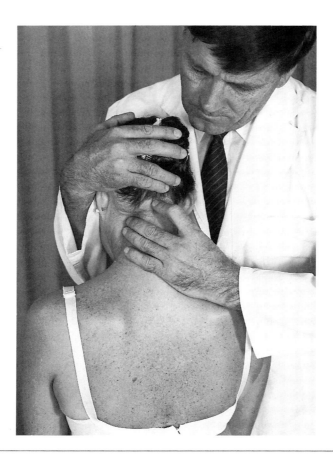

Fig. 4.8   # Method of testing flexion of the atlanto-axial complex

Patient position: Sitting.

Therapist position: Standing on the patient's right.

Hand position: The therapist takes hold of the patient's head with the right arm so that the little finger of the right hand is placed around the posterior arch of C1. The fingers of the right hand are allowed to spread over the back of the patient's head.

The therapist's left hand is placed so that the tip of the index finger is situated over the superior aspect of the spinous process of C2; the tip of the middle finger over the left articular pillar of C2; and the tip of the thumb over the right articular pillar of C2.

Movement: C1 is flexed on C2 by tilting the head and C1 forwards on C2. The movement is felt between the palpating fingers of the left hand and the movement of the arch of C1.

EXTENSION

On extension, there is an approximation of the posterior arch of the atlas and the spinous process of the axis and a gapping of the articular surfaces anteriorly.

Fig. 4.9   **Extension of the atlanto-axial complex**

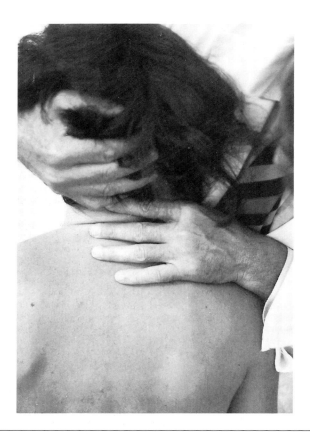

Fig. 4.10 **Method of testing extension of the atlanto-axial complex**

Patient position: Sitting.

Therapist position: Standing on the patient's right side.

Hand position: As for flexion of c1 on c2.

Movement: The head and c1 are tilted backwards on c2. The movement is felt between the palpating fingers of the left hand and the arch of c1.

ROTATION

On right rotation, of the atlas on axis, the left inferior articular surface of the atlas moves forwards on the left superior articular surface of the axis, and the right inferior articular surface of the atlas moves backwards on the right superior articular surface of the axis.

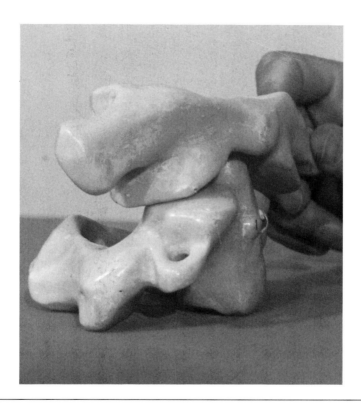

Fig. 4.11   **Right rotation of the atlanto-axial complex**

Upper cervical spine

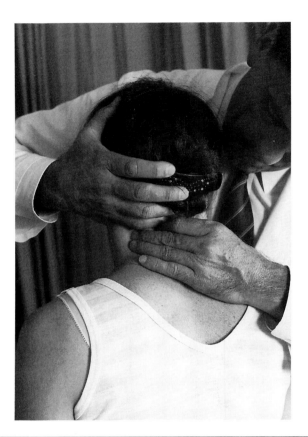

Fig. 4.12 **Method of testing right rotation of the atlanto-axial complex**

Patient position: Sitting.

Therapist position: Standing on patient's right side.

Hand position: The therapist takes hold of the patient's head with the right arm so that the little finger of the therapist's right hand is placed around the arch of c1. The fingers of the right hand are allowed to spread over the back of the patient's head. The therapist's left hand is placed so that the tip of the index finger is over the left hand side of the spinous process of the axis, and the thumb over the right hand side articulation.

Movement: The patient's head and c1 are rotated to the right. The movement of the rotation of c1 and c2 is felt between the palpating fingers of the left hand. The left articular pillar of c1 will be felt to move away from the pad of the left middle finger.

Examination of the occipito-atlantal complex using combined movements

The principles when combining movements in the high cervical spine are the same as with the rest of the vertebral column, i.e. movements are combined which tend to stretch and compress the joints and surrounding structures.

RIGHT ROTATION IN FLEXION

On flexion, the condyles of the occiput move backwards in relation to the articular surface of the atlas. If this is combined with rotation, say to the right, an increased stretch is placed on the posterior part of the capsule of the right occipito-atlantal joint.

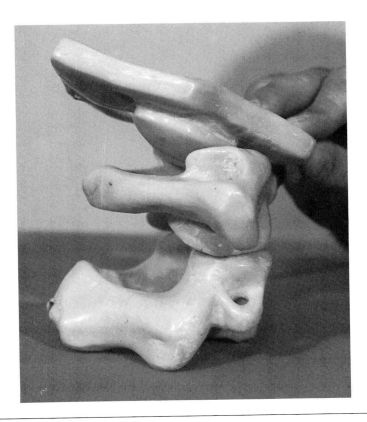

Fig. 4.13   **Right rotation in flexion of the atlanto-occipital complex**

Upper cervical spine

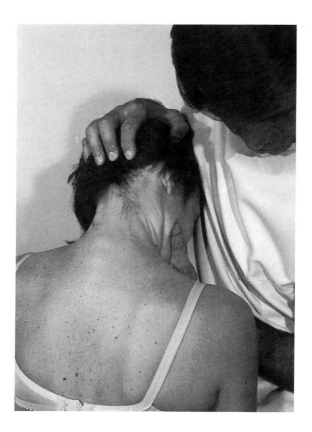

Fig. 4.14   **Method of testing right rotation in flexion of the atlanto-occipital complex**

Patient position:	Sitting.
Therapist position:	Standing in front and slightly to the side of the patient. The head is to be rotated to this side.
Hand position:	The left elbow is flexed and the left forearm supinated. The left hand cups the symphysis menti. The right forearm is placed over the crown of the head and the fingers of the right hand grip the head below the occiput but above the arch of C1.
Movement:	The head is then flexed on the neck and right rotation of the head is added, so as to stretch the posterior structures on the right between the occiput and C1.

RIGHT ROTATION IN EXTENSION

On extension, the condyles of the occiput move forwards in relation to the articular surface of the atlas. If this is combined with rotation to the right, an increase in the stretch on the anterior capsule of the occipito-atlantal joint is obtained.

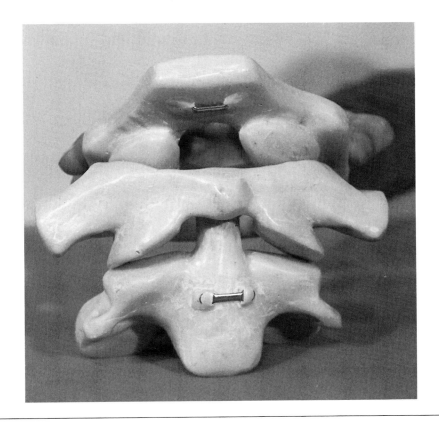

Fig. 4.15   **Right rotation in extension of the atlanto-occipital complex**

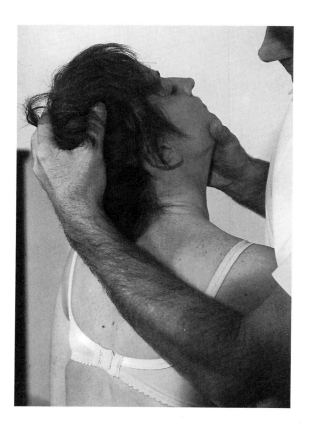

| Fig. 4.16 | **Method of testing right rotation in extension of the atlanto-occipital complex** |

Patient position: Sitting.

Therapist position: Standing in front and slightly to the patient's right.

Hand position: The therapist's right hand grasps the patient's chin. The left hand is placed over the crown of the patient's head so that the fingers rest on the patient's forehead.

Movement: The head is extended on the neck and right rotation is added so as to stretch the anterior structures between the occiput and C1 on the left.

Examination of the atlanto-axial complex using combined movements

FLEXION IN RIGHT ROTATION

On rotation to the right of the atlas on axis, the inferior articular surface of the atlas moves forward on the left superior articular surface of the axis. The opposite occurs on the right hand side. If flexion is then added, an increase in the stretch of the left and right posterior aspects of the atlanto-axial joint is obtained.

Fig. 4.17   **Flexion in right rotation of the atlanto-axial complex**

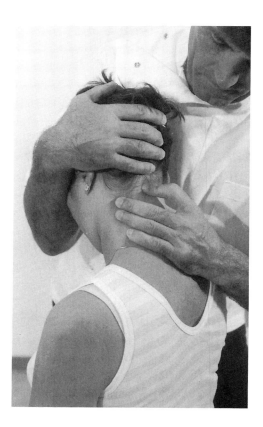

Fig. 4.18

Method of testing flexion in right rotation of the atlanto-axial complex

Patient position: Sitting.

Therapist position: Standing, facing the patient on the right hand side.

Hand position: The therapist's right arm is placed around the patient's head so that the little finger is around the arch of the atlas. The therapist's left hand is placed over the axis so that the pad of the index finger is over the spinous process of the axis; the left middle finger is placed over the left articular pillar of axis and the left thumb is placed over the right articular pillar of axis.

Movement: The head and atlas are rotated to the right and forward flexion of the head and atlas is added.

EXTENSION IN RIGHT ROTATION

On rotation to the right of the atlas on axis, the inferior articular surface of the atlas moves forwards on the left superior articular surface of the axis, and the opposite occurs on the right hand side. If extension is added, there is an increase in the stretch on the right and left anterior parts of the capsule of the atlanto-axial joint.

Fig. 4.19   **Extension in right rotation of the atlanto-axial complex**

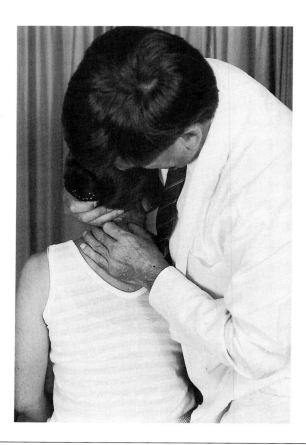

| Fig. 4.20 | **Method of testing extension in right rotation of the atlanto-axial complex** |

Patient position: Sitting.

Therapist position: Standing facing the patient on the right hand side.

Hand position: As for right rotation and flexion.

Movement: The head and atlas are rotated to the right on the axis and extension of the head and atlas is added.

Confirmation by palpation

The passive testing procedures described above will elicit signs which are related more to restriction than reproduction of pain. Thus, following the examination of physiological movements, the next step is to either confirm the findings by palpation or, where the appropriate symptoms have not been reproduced by combined movements, they must be found with palpation. Very often, specific signs and symptoms will be more easily isolated by palpation.

When carrying out the techniques of palpation, close attention must be paid, by placing the joint to be examined in the appropriate combined position. This position must be strongly maintained while the palpation procedure is performed.

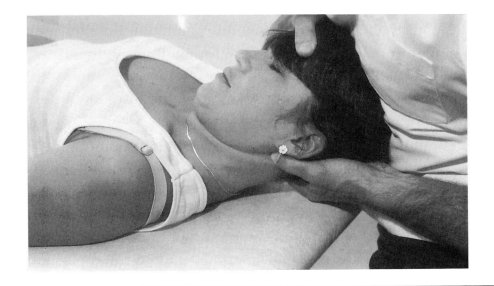

Fig. 4.21	**Anterior pressure on the left of the atlas, with the head flexed and rotated to the left**

Patient position: Supine.

Therapist position: Standing at the patient's head.

Hand position: The therapist's right hand is placed over the patient's forehead so that the fingers of the hand are down over the right lateral aspect of the patient's forehead. The therapist's left hand is placed under the occiput, allowing the pad of the left thumb to be placed over the anterior aspect of the left transverse process of C1.

Movement: The patient's head is maintained in a position of flexion and left rotation and anterior pressure is applied over the left transverse process of C1, so as to decrease stretch on the posterior structures on the left between occiput and atlas.

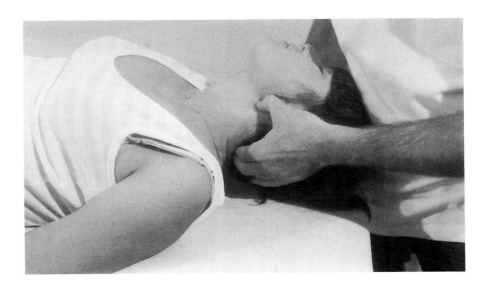

Fig. 4.22   **Anterior pressure on the left of the atlas, with the head
                        extended and rotated to the right**

Patient position: Supine, with the head in a position of extension and right rotation.

Therapist position: Standing at the patient's head.

Hand position: Both hands cradle the patient's head so that both index fingers lie along
                        the arch of C1. The pad of the left thumb is placed over the anterior aspect
                        of the left transverse process of C1.

Movement: The patient's head is extended over the therapist's index fingers and right
                        rotation is added. The left thumb applies anterior pressure on the left
                        transverse process of C1.

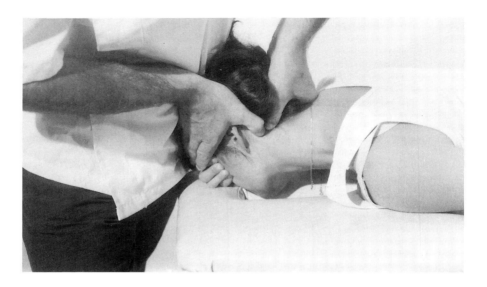

| Fig. 4.23 | **Posterior pressure on the left of the atlas, with the head extended and rotated to the right** |

Patient position: Prone, with right hand cupped over the forehead. The head is extended and rotated to the right.

Therapist position: Standing at the patient's head and slightly to the patient's right.

Hand position: The therapist's right forearm is flexed and the right wrist is extended. The fingers of the right hand are placed over the patient's left parietal area. The therapist's right thumb is extended at the metacarpo-phalangeal joint and flexed at the interphalangeal joint, so that the tip of the right thumb is placed over the posterior aspect of the patient's left transverse process of C1. The therapist's left hand is placed over the posterior aspect of the patient's cervical spine so that the tip of the abducted left thumb is placed over the posterior aspect of the left transverse process of C1. The fingers of the left hand are allowed to spread over the right hand side of the patient's cervical spine.

Movement: The head is maintained in a position of extension and right rotation. Posterior pressure is carried out over the left transverse process of C1 so as to decrease the stretch on the left anterior structures between occiput and C1.

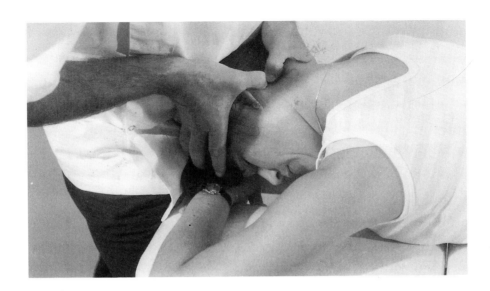

| Fig. 4.24 | **Posterior pressure over the left transverse process of the atlas, with the head and atlas rotated to the left and flexed on the axis** |

Patient position:	Prone, with the head and atlas rotated to the left and flexed. The patient's forehead is rested on the dorsal aspect of the left hand.
Therapist position:	Standing at the patient's head.
Hand position:	The tips of the therapist's opposed thumbs are placed over the posterior aspect of the left transverse process of atlas. The fingers of the right hand are spread over the patient's temporal area, and those of the left over the right lateral aspect of the patient's cervical spine.
Movement:	The head and atlas are maintained in a position of flexion and left rotation while posterior pressure is applied over the left transverse process of atlas. This decreases the rotation between atlas and axis.

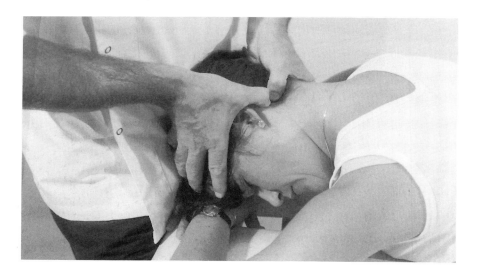

| Fig. 4.25 | **Posterior pressure over the left lateral mass of the axis, with the head and atlas rotated to the left and flexed on the axis** |

Patient position: Prone, with the head and atlas rotated to left and flexed on axis.

Therapist position: Standing at the patient's head.

Hand position: The tips of the therapist's opposed thumbs are placed over the left lateral mass of axis; the fingers of the right hand are placed over the patient's left temporal area and those of the left on the right lateral aspect of the patient's cervical spine.

Movement: The head and atlas are maintained in a position of left rotation and flexion while posterior pressure is applied to the left lateral mass of axis. This increases the rotation to the left between axis and atlas.

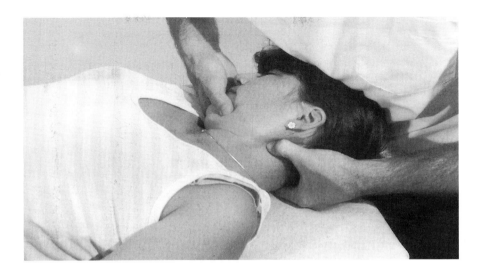

| Fig. 4.26 | **Anterior pressure over the left of the axis, with the head and atlas rotated to the right and flexed on the axis** |

Patient position: Supine, with the head and atlas in flexion and right rotation.

Therapist position: Standing at the head of the patient.

Hand position: The web of the therapist's right hand is placed over the patient's chin so that the right thumb is placed over the left mandible and the fingers of the right hand are allowed to spread over the right mandible. The therapist's left hand is placed so that the pad of the left thumb is placed over the anterior aspect of the lateral mass of axis.

Movement: The head and atlas are maintained in the flexed and rotated position while anterior pressure is applied on the left lateral mass of the axis, so as to increase the rotation between axis and atlas.

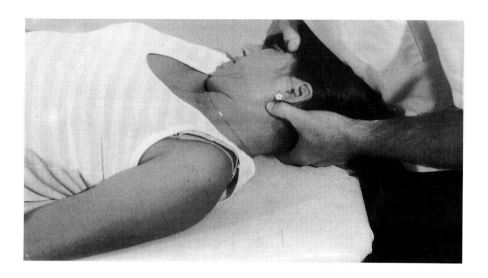

| Fig. 4.27 | **Anterior pressure over the left of the atlas, with the head and atlas rotated to the right and flexed on the axis** |

Patient position: Supine. The head and atlas are rotated to the right and flexed on the axis.

Therapist position: Standing at the head of the patient.

Hand position: The therapist's right hand is placed over the patient's forehead so as to maintain the position of flexion and right rotation. The therapist's left hand is placed so that the pad of the left thumb is placed over the anterior aspect of the transverse process of atlas.

Movement: Anterior pressure is applied over the anterior aspect of the transverse process of the atlas, so as to decrease the rotation between atlas and axis.

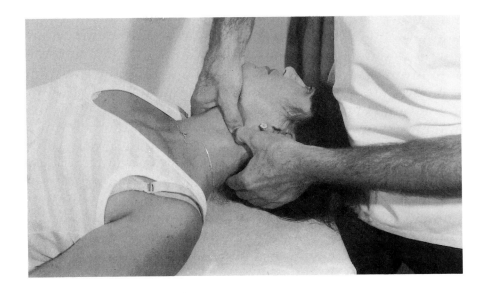

| Fig. 4.28 | **Anterior pressure on the left of the axis, with the head and atlas rotated to the right and extended on the axis** |

Patient position: Supine, with the head and atlas rotated to the right on the axis.

Therapist position: Standing at the patient's head.

Hand position: The dorsal aspect of the tip of each thumb is placed in opposition over the anterior aspect of the left articular pillar of the axis. The fingers of the right hand are placed over the right hand side of the patient's cervical spine; those of the left are placed around the arch of the atlas and occiput.

Movement: The head and atlas are maintained in a position of right rotation and extension and anterior pressure is applied to the left of the axis. This pressure will tend to increase the effect of the rotation between atlas and axis.

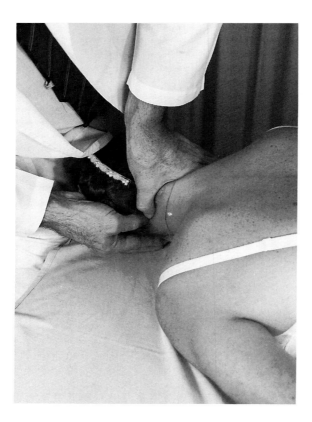

Fig. 4.29

Posterior pressure over the left transverse process of the atlas, with the head and atlas rotated to the right and flexed on the axis

Patient position: Prone, with the head and atlas rotated to the right and flexed. The patient's forehead is rested on the dorsal aspect of the patient's right hand.

Therapist position: Standing at the patient's head.

Hand position: The tips of the opposed thumbs are placed over the posterior aspect of the left transverse process of the atlas. The fingers of the right hand are spread over the patient's temporal area, and those of the left over the right lateral aspect of the patient's cervical spine.

Movement: The head and atlas are maintained in a position of flexion and right rotation while posterior pressure is applied over the left transverse process of the atlas. This increases the rotation between atlas and axis.

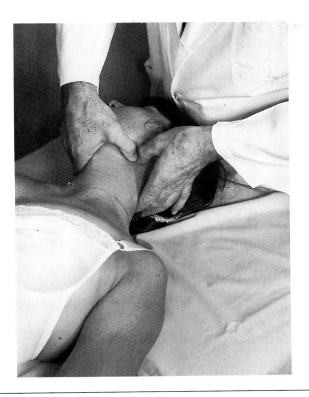

Fig. 4.30

Anterior pressure on the left transverse process of the atlas, with the head and atlas rotated to the right and extended on the axis

Patient position: Supine, with the head and atlas extended and rotated to the right on the axis.

Therapist position: Standing at the head of the patient.

Hand position: The tips of the thumbs are placed in a position over the anterior aspect of the transverse process of the atlas. The fingers of the right hand are allowed to spread over the right hand side of the patient's cervical spine, and those of the left around the occiput.

Movement: Anterior pressure is applied over the left transverse process of the atlas so as to decrease the rotation between atlas and axis.

REFERENCE

Brakman R, Penning L 1971 Injuries of the cervical spine. In: Excerpta Medica, Amsterdam, ch 1, p 3–30

5. Middle and lower cervical spine and thoracic spine

Objective Examination of the Middle and Lower Cervical Spine

SPECIFIC MOVEMENTS AND OBSERVATIONS

The patient needs to be sufficiently undressed to allow observation of the upper body, as well as the upper limbs, and to allow the performance of a full neurological examination. Whilst it is usual to examine the patient in the sitting position, it may be worth performing the initial observations with the patient standing as this makes it easier to see certain features, such as spinal deformity.

Observation from behind

When observing from behind, the following may be seen and variation noted:

1. Altered shoulder height
2. Obvious changes in muscle tone of the muscles of the shoulders and neck
3. Position of the head and neck on the shoulders
4. Position of the scapulae.

Observation from in front

When observing from the front, the clinician should take note of the following features:

1. Level of the clavicles
2. Obvious changes in the tone of the anterior cervical musculature
3. Protraction or retraction of the shoulder girdle.

Observation from the side

When observing from the side, the clinician should be aware of:

1. Position of the head in relation to the neck
2. Position of the neck and head in relation to the thoracic spine
3. Shape of the cervical, thoracic and lumbar spinal curves (any increased or decreased kyphosis or lordosis)
4. Posture while sitting.

EXAMINATION OF MOVEMENTS

The cervical spine can be examined with the therapist standing either in front of or behind the patient. Examination from behind allows the therapist to observe the segmental movement of the cervical joints. Examination while standing in front of the patient allows a good view of facial expression, and facial features can be used as landmarks in judging changes in range of movement.

Middle and lower cervical spine and thoracic spine

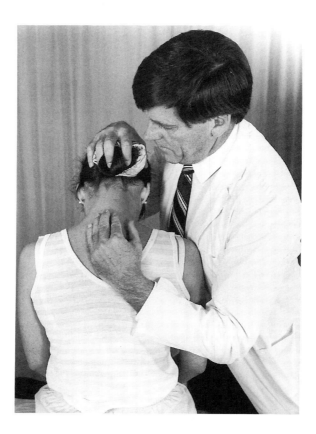

Fig 5.1   **Examination of flexion**

Patient position: Sitting.

Therapist position: Standing to the side and slightly in front of the patient.

Hand position: The therapist's right hand is placed over the patient's head so that the fingers of the right hand rest below the axis. The right forearm is placed over the crown of the head. The therapist's left hand is placed so that the palm is over the upper thoracic spine and the middle, index and ring fingers are placed to the centre, right and left of T1 respectively.

Movement: The head and neck are flexed with the therapist's right hand and the upper thoracic spine is stabilized with the left hand.

After ascertaining the area of symptoms, the patient is asked to bend the head forwards as far as possible, attempting to put the head on to the chest.

The range at which the symptoms occur or change is noted and any deviation from the median plane or abnormality of segmental movement is observed. As with the lumbar spine, the return from the flexed position is assessed and note taken of an arc of pain, if present. Taking the C4/5 joint as an example: at the zygapophyseal joint, during the movement of flexion, the inferior articular facets of C4 will slide superiorly on the superior articular facets of C5.

Middle and lower cervical spine and thoracic spine

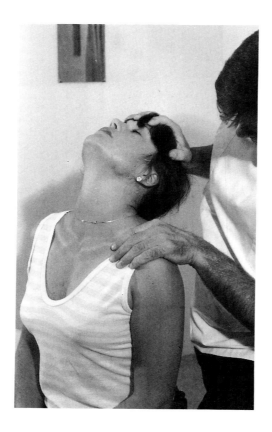

Fig 5.2	# Examination of extension

Patient position: Sitting.

Therapist position: Standing behind the patient.

Hand position: The therapist's right hand is placed over the crown of the patient's head. The therapist's left hand takes hold of the patient's left shoulder.

Movement: The patient is asked to extend the head, and movement is assisted by the therapist.

The patient is asked to extend the neck and note is taken of any deviation in the path of the movement and of intersegmental movement. During this movement, again using C4/5 as an example, the inferior facet of C4 will slide inferiorly on the superior facet of C5.

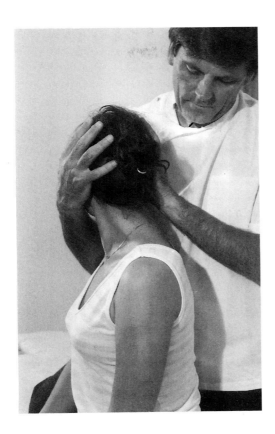

Fig 5.3	# Examination of right rotation

Patient position:	Sitting.
Therapist position:	Standing on patient's right side and facing the patient's back.
Hand position:	The therapist's right hand is placed around the patient's left zygomatic arch and the fingers spread over the left temporal region. The therapist's left hand is placed over the right temporal region.
Movement:	Active assisted movement of right rotation is carried out.

The patient is asked to look over his/her shoulder. It is important to observe the posterior joints and musculature carefully and to attempt to identify any abnormalities of movement. During rotation, the right inferior facet of C4 will slide down in relation to the right superior facet of C5. The opposite will occur at the left joints, with the inferior facet of C4 sliding upwards in relation to the superior articular facet of C5.

Middle and lower cervical spine and thoracic spine

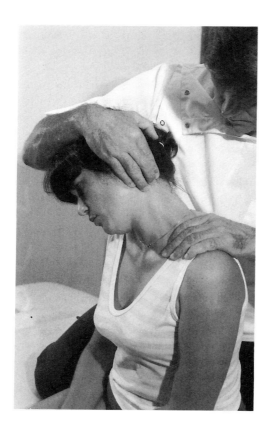

| Fig 5.4 | **Examination of right lateral flexion** |

Patient position: Sitting.

Therapist position: Standing on the patient's right hand side.

Hand position: The therapist's right forearm and hand is placed over the patient's head so that the index finger of the right hand comes below the lateral mass of the axis. The therapist's left hand is placed over the patient's left suprascapular fossa and left clavicle.

Movement: Lateral flexion to the right is performed by moving the cervical spine to the right and stabilizing with the left hand.

When asking the patient to tip the head to the side, it may be useful, when adding overpressure, to use the side of one's hand to localize the movement to the level possibly responsible for the symptoms. As with lateral flexion in the lumbar spine, it is possible to observe intersegmental movement, especially comparing the movement that occurs at the posterior joints during left lateral flexion compared to right lateral flexion. The movement that occurs at the zygapophyseal joints is similar to that which occurs during rotation, with 'closing' of the ipsilateral joints and 'opening' of the contralateral joints.

Examination of Combined Movements

MECHANICAL PRINCIPLES

In the middle (c3–5) cervical spine, the movements of rotation and lateral flexion occur together. It seems most likely that these movements occur in the same direction. Lateral flexion to the right is combined with rotation to the right (Stoddard 1969). This is at least partly due to the shape of the joint surfaces, but this movement is also affected by the soft tissue structures between the bony articulations and the structures between the neural foramina and vertebral canal. Different movements of the cervical spine, e.g. flexion with lateral flexion in one direction and rotation in the same direction, can cause stretching or compressing effects of the intervertebral joints on either side.

When flexion is performed in the sagittal plane, the articular surfaces of the zygapophyseal joint slide on one another, with the inferior articular facet of the superior vertebra sliding cephalad on the superior articular facet of the inferior vertebra, while at the same time the interbody space is narrowed anteriorly and widened posteriorly. Rotation to the left and left lateral flexion cause the right zygapophyseal facet to open. While these movements of lateral flexion and rotation result in a similar upward motion of the superior on the inferior facet, they are not identical movements.

Consider the movements of the cervical spine in relation to the facet joints. With the movement of lateral flexion and rotation to the right, e.g. of the fourth cervical vertebra (c4) on the fifth (c5), the right inferior facet of c4 slides down the right superior facet of c5. A similar movement on the right side occurs in extension. Therefore, there is some similarity in terms of direction of movement of the right facet joint in the movements of extension, right lateral flexion and right rotation. The facet joint on the opposite side moves upward during each movement (except with extension).

Because of the combination of movements which occur in the cervical spine, the examination of the patients' movements must be expanded to incorporate these principles. In other words, there are times when it is inadequate to examine the basic movements of flexion, extension, lateral flexion and rotation, and other movements combining these basic movements must be examined. The symptoms and signs which are produced by examining rotary or lateral flexion movements performed while the spine is maintained in the neutral position in relation to other movements can be quite different to the signs and symptoms produced when the same movements are performed with the spine in flexion or extension. Testing movements while the spine is maintained in flexion or extension can cause symptoms to be accentuated, reduced or may even change the symptoms, from producing local spinal pain to producing referred pain.

The range of movement possible when producing movements in the neutral position will be different to that obtained when movements are performed in combined positions. For example, the range of either rotation or lateral flexion may be greater when the movement is performed in the neutral position compared to the amount of rotation possible when the movement is being performed in the fully flexed position. As well as differences in range of movement, there is also much greater stretch or compression of structures on either side.

Middle and lower cervical spine and thoracic spine

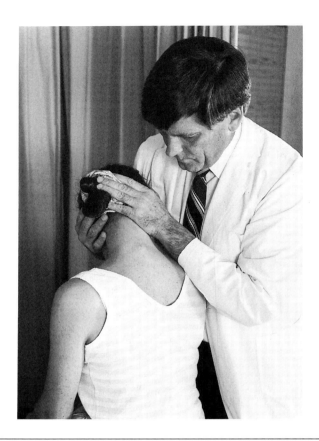

Fig 5.5	# Examination of right rotation in flexion

Patient position: Sitting.

Therapist position: Standing on the right hand side into the back of the patient.

Hand position: As for right rotation.

Movement: Active assisted movement of flexion and then right rotation is carried out.

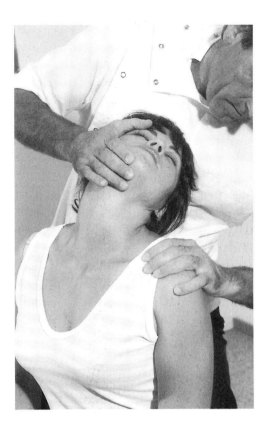

Fig 5.6   # Examination of left rotation in extension

Patient position: Sitting.

Therapist position: Standing on the patient's right hand side and to the back.

Hand position: The therapist's right hand is placed so that the fingers are under the patient's chin. The left hand is placed over the patient's left shoulder.

Movement: Active assisted movement of extension and then left rotation is carried out.

Middle and lower cervical spine and thoracic spine

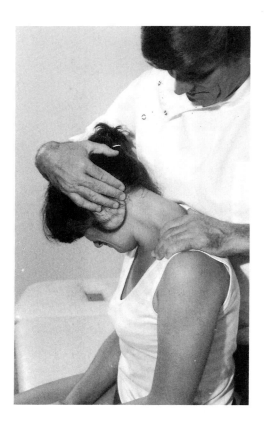

| Fig 5.7 | **Examination of right lateral flexion in flexion** |

Patient position: Sitting.

Therapist position: Standing on the patient's right hand side and to the back.

Hand position: The therapist's right hand is placed over the crown of the patient's head so that the fingers come down to cover the patient's left ear. The left hand is placed over the patient's left suprascapular fossa.

Movement: Active assisted movement of forward flexion and right lateral flexion.

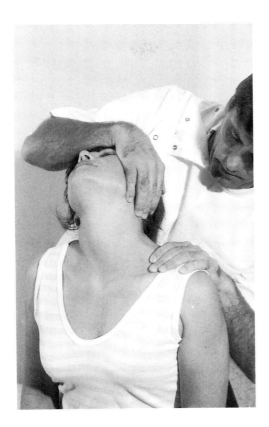

Fig 5.8   # Examination of right lateral flexion in extension

Patient position: Sitting.

Therapist position: Standing to the back and to the patient's right side.

Hand position: The therapist' right hand is placed over the patient's forehead so that the fingers of the right hand come down to the level of the transverse process of C2. The left hand is placed over the patient's left shoulder.

Movement: Active assisted movement of extension and right lateral flexion.

Physiological Treatment Techniques

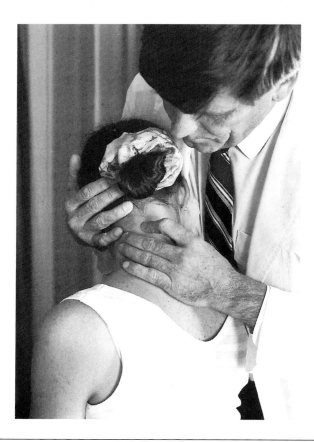

Fig 5.9	**Right rotation in flexion**

Patient position: Sitting.

Therapist position: Standing on the patient's right hand side.

Hand position: The therapist's right hand is placed so that the pad of the right little finger is placed on the left inferior facet articulation of the vertebra above. The therapist's left hand is placed so that the pad of the left index finger is placed over the left hand side of the spinous process of the vertebra below, the left middle finger over the left superior facet of the vertebra below and the left thumb over the right superior facet of the vertebra below.

Movement: Rotation to the right of the left facet joint in flexion is performed by the therapist's right hand, while fixation of lower vertebra is maintained with the left hand.

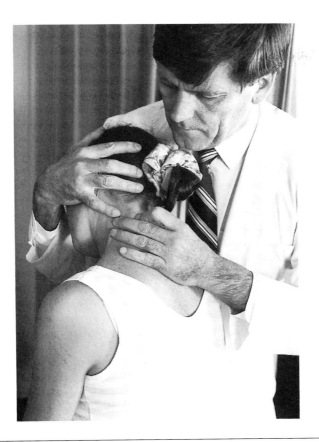

Fig 5.10   **Right lateral flexion in flexion**

Patient position: Sitting.

Therapist position: Standing on the patient's right side.

Hand position: As for right rotation in flexion.

Movement: The head and neck are right laterally flexed with the right hand, while stabilization of the vertebra below is maintained with the left hand.

Middle and lower cervical spine and thoracic spine

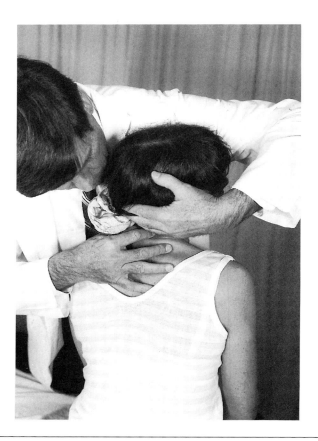

Fig 5.11   **Right rotation in extension**

Patient position: Sitting.

Therapist position: Standing on the patient's left side.

Hand position: The therapist's left hand is placed so that the pad of the left little finger is placed over the right inferior facet of the vertebra above. The pad of the therapist's right thumb is placed over the left hand side of the spinous process of the vertebra below.

Movement: The head and neck are rotated to the right in extension while fixation of the vertebra below is maintained with the right hand.

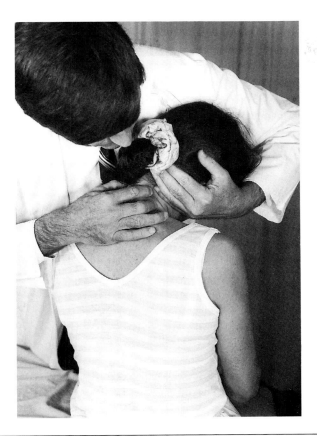

Fig 5.12	**Right rotation in flexion — alternative method**

Patient position: Sitting.

Therapist position: Standing on the patient's left hand side.

Hand position: As for right rotation in extension.

Movement: Right rotation of the head and neck in flexion is performed with the therapist's left hand, while fixation of the vertebra below is maintained with the therapist's right hand.

Middle and lower cervical spine and thoracic spine

Use of accessory movements (confirmation by palpation)

As with the high cervical spine, signs found on physiological movements can be confirmed by palpation. If, for example, right sided middle cervical pain occurs with right rotation, and this pain is accentuated when right rotation is performed in extension, these findings may be confirmed by comparing responses to anterior and posterior palpation. Using this example, and assuming an articular problem between c4 and c5, anterior pressure on the right, directed caudally over the anterior tubercle of c4, will increase the symptoms; whereas anterior pressure on the right directed caudally over c5 will decrease the symptoms. A comparison of these findings with those found by posterior palpation is useful. Posterior palpation directed caudally over the right inferior articulation of c4 will increase the symptoms, while posterior pressure directed caudally over the right superior articulation of c5 will decrease the symptoms.

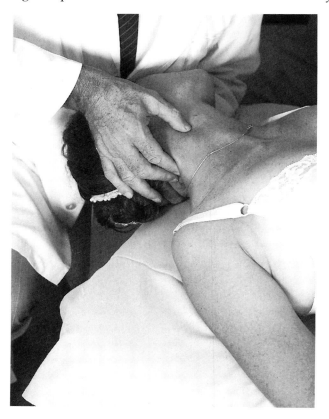

Fig 5.13   **Anterior palpation on the right with the neck in left rotation and extension**

Patient position: Lying supine with the head in extension and left rotation.

Therapist position: Standing at the patient's head.

Hand position: The therapist's hands cradle the patient's head and neck. The therapist's right thumb is placed anteriorly over the inferior articulation of the vertebra above, or anteriorly over the superior articulation of the vertebra below, the level to be tested.

Movement: Anteroposterior direction.

Middle and lower cervical spine and thoracic spine

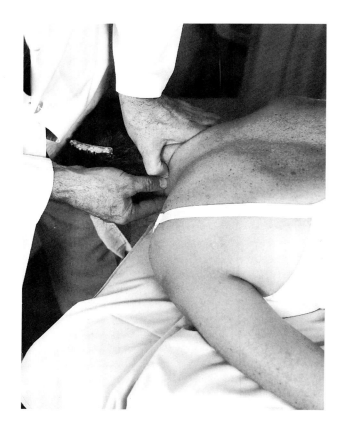

Fig 5.14

Posterior palpation on the left with the neck in flexion and right rotation

Patient position: Prone, with the head flexed and rotated to the right.

Therapist position: Standing at the head of the patient.

Hand position: The therapist's hands are placed so that the thumbs are over the left posterior articulation of the inferior articulation of the vertebra above, or the superior articulation of the vertebra below.

Movement: Posterio-anterior direction.

c6–t1 Accessory Movements

Examination and technique in this area is the same as for the middle cervical spine, except that examination of the first rib is included.

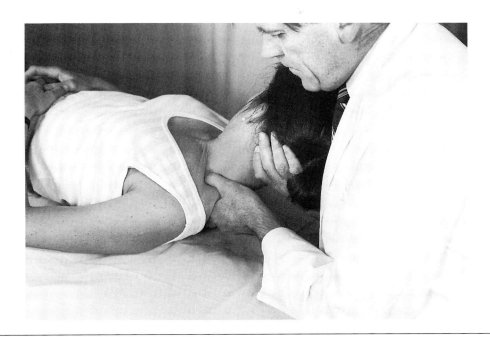

Fig 5.15   **Caudad pressure of the left first rib, with the lower cervical spine in flexion and right rotation**

Patient position: Supine.

Therapist position: Standing at the head of the patient.

Hand position: The therapist's right hand takes hold of the patient's head, grasping the head and neck below c2. The lower cervical spine is then flexed and rotated to the right. The therapist's left thumb is placed over the patient's left first rib.

Movement: Caudad movement of first rib with therapist's left thumb.

Thoracic Spine

The same principles described for the middle and low cervical spine apply in the thoracic spine. The attached ribs need to be included in the mobilizing procedures.

As a general principle, when a rib is fixed, mobilization by rotation of the adjacent vertebrae to the same side increases the effect of the fixation on that side.

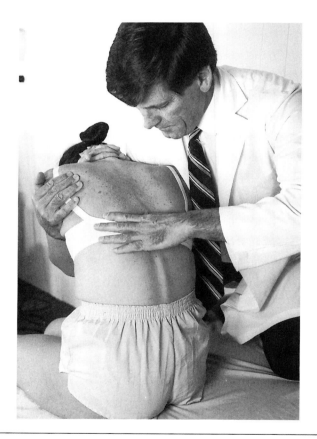

Fig 5.16   **Right rotation in flexion**

Patient position: Sitting, hands clasped behind neck.

Therapist position: Standing on the patient's right side.

Hand position: The therapist's right arm is placed through the patient's linked arms so that the patient's right shoulder is in the therapist's right axilla. The therapist's right hand takes hold of the patient's left shoulder. The therapist's left hand is placed so that the pad of the left thumb is placed over the left hand side of the spinous process of the vertebra below. The left index finger fixes the adjacent rib.

Movement: Right rotation in flexion is carried out with the right arm and hand, while flexion is maintained with the left.

Middle and lower cervical spine and thoracic spine

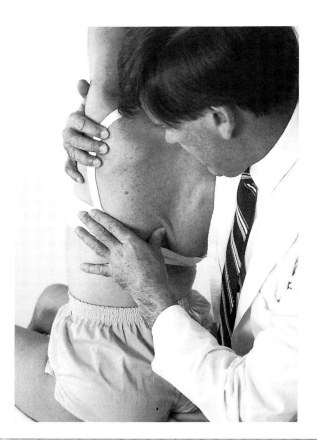

Fig 5.17   **Right rotation in extension**

Patient position: Sitting.

Therapist position: Standing on the patient's right side.

Hand position: As for right rotation in flexion.

Movement: Rotation to the right in extension is performed with the therapist's right hand and arm, while extension is maintained with the therapist's left hand and index finger.

Fig 5.18   **Unilateral pressure on the left, with the thoracic spine in flexion and right rotation**

Patient position: As for flexion and right rotation.

Therapist position: Standing.

Hand position: The therapist's thumbs are placed forward over the left transverse process of the vertebra to be mobilized.

Movement: Posterior anterior movement over the left transverse process.

REFERENCES

Stoddard A 1969 Manual of osteopathic practice. Hutchinson, London

6. Movement patterns

The movements of the vertebral column are complex and, as yet, not fully understood. The articulations are such that each vertebral segment, when moved, involves movement of 3 different joints: the two zygapophyseal joints and the disc. In the cervical spine, the uncovertebral joints of Luschka also play a part, while in the thoracic spine, movements are complicated further by the articulations of the ribs. As well as the shape of the articulations, the amount and type of movement which is possible at each level is affected by the soft tissue structures between the bony articulations and the structures within the neural foramina and vertebral canal.

The movements of the vertebral column do not occur in isolation but rather in a combined manner. Some aspects of this have already been investigated (Farfan 1975, Loebl 1973, Rolander 1966, Stoddard 1969). Others have found that axial rotation of the lumbar spine was to the left when the subject bent to the left and to the right when bending to the right. However, they did find that in one subject, the reverse was the case. Stoddard (1969) states that the direction of rotation during lateral flexion in the lumbar and thoracic spine will vary depending on whether the lateral flexion is performed with the whole of the spine in flexion or extension. He suggests that the rotation is to the same side as the lateral flexion when the movement of lateral flexion is performed in flexion, but to the opposite side when the movement is performed in extension (Stoddard 1969).

There appears to be little dispute as to the direction of rotation in the cervical spine (C2–C7). This has been investigated by a number of authors (Kapandji 1974, Lysell 1969, Mesdagh 1976, Parke 1975, Penning 1978). The direction of rotation appears to be the same regardless of whether the movement of lateral flexion is performed in flexion or extension. The investigations so far appear to show that the combination of lateral flexion and rotation being always to the same side relates to the effect on the zygapophyseal joints and disc. However, as mentioned previously, the involvement of soft tissue, muscle, ligaments and structures within the canal and foramina all play a part in the type of movement possible at each level.

Because of the combination of movement which occurs in the vertebral column, the examination of a patient's movements can, and sometimes must, be expanded to incorporate these principles. In other words, there are times when to examine the basic movements of flexion, extension, lateral flexion and rotation is inadequate; on these occasions, other movements combining these basic movements must be examined.

The symptoms and signs which are produced by examining rotary or lateral flexion movements, performed while the spine is maintained in the neutral position in relation to other movements, can be quite different from the symptoms and signs produced when the same movements are performed with the spine in flexion or extension. Testing movements while the spine is maintained in flexion and extension can cause symptoms to be accentuated, reduced or it may change the symptoms from the production of local spinal pain to the production of referred pain.

EXAMINATION OF ROTARY AND LATERAL FLEXION MOVEMENTS

Examination of rotary and lateral flexion movements in varying positions of flexion and extension helps to establish the type of movement pattern present. Combining movements gives an indication as to the way signs and symptoms change, when the same movement is performed in flexion and extension. For example, the amount of rotation which is possible between c2 and c3 will vary depending on the amount of flexion or extension present when the movement is performed. Similarly, in the lumbar spine, the amount of lateral flexion may vary depending on the amount of flexion or extension in which the movement is performed. Because of the above, the symptoms produced by testing movements of rotation in the cervical spine and lateral flexion in the lumbar spine may vary quite considerably, depending on whether the movements are performed in some degree of flexion or extension.

This same principle, of course, applies to other combinations of movements. Left rotation of, say, the cervical spine may produce left supra-scapular fossa pain when the rotation is performed in the neutral position. This pain may be accentuated, however, when the same movement is performed in extension and eased when done in flexion. In the lumbar spine, left lateral flexion may produce left buttock pain when the movement is performed in the neutral position; however the pain may be accentuated when the movement is performed in extension and eased when performed in flexion.

The movements described above involve the combining of 2 movements. However, the combining of three movements may also be performed. For example, lateral flexion and rotation can be carried out either in flexion or extension. These movements can be performed in any section of the spine. It is also vital to realize that the sequence of performing the movements may be varied and produce different symptomatic responses. This is because the movement which is performed first can reduce the available range of the second movement; and obviously the available range of the third movement is restricted even further. When using these combinations of movements as examining movements, care must be taken to ensure that each position is maintained while performing the next movement. An idea of the possible variations of sequence can be seen in this example of lateral flexion and rotation to the left of the cervical spine.

1. Flexion first, then lateral flexion to the left second and rotation to the left third.
2. Flexion first, rotation to the left second and lateral flexion to the left third.
3. Lateral flexion to the left first, flexion second and rotation to the left third.
4. Lateral flexion to the left first, rotation to the left second and flexion third.
5. Rotation to the left first, flexion second and lateral flexion to the left third.
6. Rotation to the left first, lateral flexion to the left second and flexion to the left third.

Different movements of the spine — those in flexion, lateral flexion one way and rotation one way — can cause similar stretching or compressing movements on the side of the intervertebral joint. When flexion is performed in the sagittal plane, the articular surfaces of the zygapophyseal joints slide on one another, the inferior articular facets of the superior vertebrae sliding cephalad on the superior articular facets of the inferior vertebrae. At the same time, the interbody space is narrowed anteriorly and widened posteriorly. This causes an opening movement which is similar on the right side of the intervertebral joint. It is important to state that the movement is similar in that it is an opening movement on the right, but that it is not an *identical* movement.

Combining movements of examination can therefore increase or decrease compressive or stretch effects on an intervertebral segment. This results in recognizable patterns in patients with mechanical disorders of movement. These are:

a. regular, and
b. irregular, patterns of movement.

Regular patterns

These are patterns in which similar movements at the intervertebral joint produce the same symptoms whenever the movements are performed. The symptoms, however, may differ in quality or severity. Regular patterns can further be subdivided into *compressing* or *stretching* patterns. If the patient's symptoms are produced on the side to which the movement is directed, then the pattern is a compressing pattern, i.e. the compressing movements produce the symptoms. If the symptoms are present on the opposite side from that to which the movement is directed, then the pattern can be considered a stretching pattern. The following are examples of regular compressing patterns.

1. Right cervical rotation produces right suprascapular pain. This pain is made worse when the same movement is performed in extension and eased when performed in flexion.
2. Cervical extension produces right suprascapular pain. This pain is made worse when right rotation is added to the extension and increased further when right lateral flexion is added.
3. Right lateral flexion in the lumbar spine produces right buttock pain. This is made worse when the movement is performed in extension and eased when performed in flexion.

The following are examples of regular stretching patterns.

1. Right lateral flexion in the cervical spine produces left suprascapular pain. This pain is accentuated when the same movement is performed in flexion and eased when performed in extension.
2. Flexion of the cervical spine produces left suprascapular pain. This pain is made worse when right lateral flexion is added and increased further when right rotation is added.
3. Right lateral flexion in the lumbar spine produces left buttock pain. This is accentuated when the movement of right lateral flexion is performed in flexion, and eased when right lateral flexion is performed in extension.

It must not be assumed that the simple explanation (above) is necessarily universal. The biomechanics of spinal movement are complex and have not been fully described. Influences such as changing instantaneous axes of rotation complicate the situation. The explanation conveyed in this discussion refers to simple physiological patterns of movement, and to those patterns in association with accessory movements, e.g. pain and restriction of movement on extension of the lower cervical spine being matched by similar restriction with posterior/anterior pressure over the spinous process of C5.

Irregular patterns

All patterns which are not regular as defined above fall into the category of irregular patterns. With irregular patterns, there is not the same consistency of symptoms as described, and stretching and compressing movements do not follow any recognizable pattern. There does not appear to be a regular relationship between the examination findings obtained when combining movements with either the compressing or stretching components of the movements. Rather, there is an apparent random reproduction of symptoms despite the combining of movements which have similar stretching and compressing effects on the structures on either side of the spine.

Examples of an irregular pattern of movement are as follows.

1. Right rotation of the cervical spine produces right suprascapular pain (a compressing test movement). This pain is made worse when right rotation is performed in flexion (a stretching movement) and eased when the movement is performed in extension (a compressing movement).
2. Extension of the lumbar spine increases right buttock pain. When right lateral flexion is combined with this movement, the pain is decreased, but when left lateral flexion is combined with extension, the pain is increased.

There are many examples of irregular patterns and the combinations of movements frequently indicate that there is more than one component to the disorder, e.g. the zygapophyseal joint, the interbody joint and the canal and foraminal structures may all contribute to the symptoms. Generally, traumatic injuries, e.g. whiplash and other traumatic causes of pain, do not have regular patterns of movement. Non-traumatic zygapophyseal and interbody joint disorders tend to have regular patterns of movement.

REFERENCES

Farfan H F 1975 Muscular mechanism of the lumbar spine and the position of power and efficiency. Orthopaedic Clinics of North America 6(1): 135–144

Kapandji A I 1974 Trunk and vertebral column. In: The physiology of the joints vol 3, 2nd edn. Churchill Livingstone, London

Loebl WY 1973 Regional rotation of the spine. Rheumatology and Rehabilitation 12: 223

Lysell E 1969 Motion of the cervical spine. Acta Orthopaedica Scandinavica Supp. no. 123

Mesdagh H 1976 Morphological aspects and biomechanical properties of the vertebroaxial joint (C2–3). Acta Morphologica Neerlando–Scandinavica

Parke W A 1975 Applied anatomy of the spine. In: The spine vol. 1. Saunders, Philadephia, p 19–47

Penning L 1978 Normal movements of the cervical spine. American Journal of Roentgenology 130: 317–326

Rolander S D 1966 Motion of the lumbar spine with special reference to the stabilizing effect of posterior fusion. Acta Orthopaedica Scandinavica, Supp. no. 90

Stoddard A 1969 Manual of osteopathic practice. Hutchinson, London

7. Selection of Technique

The selection of manual therapy technique remains one of the most difficult areas of treatment by passive movement. Previous authors (Grieve 1988, Maitland 1986) have addressed this problem and have based their approach on the accurate appreciation of range of movement, spasm and distribution of symptoms. The selection is also dependent upon the valuable concept of graded movement.

Although consideration must be given to the above parameters when using combined movements, the issue of the *position* of the joint is the dominant feature, as the 'grade' is always towards the end of the available range, i.e. the joint is in a position, which upon movement examination, results in either an increase or a decrease in the symptoms of which the patient is complaining. The choice of this position depends on the category of the patient; this is discussed later in the chapter. Progression of the technique is related closely to changing the position of the joint towards the position which highlights the patient's symptoms, the grade of movement technique tending to remain the same.

On initial examination, performed in the neutral position, the *primary movement* is selected, i.e. the movement which reproduces most prominently the symptoms of which the patient complains. The primary movement is then combined with the other movements of examination, e.g. if flexion is the primary movement, it is then combined with lateral flexion and rotation. The primary movement needs to be performed as a first and last part of the combination, e.g. if flexion is the primary movement, lateral flexion can be performed in flexion, and then flexion can be performed in lateral flexion. The reason for this is to establish the *primary combination*. The primary movement (PM) and the primary combination (PC) can be pictorially represented by a box diagram.

This simple diagram allows movement in all directions to be displayed. It must be understood that the diagram is drawn assuming the examining therapist is standing behind the patient, and the quadrants A, B and C, D simply refer to anterior and posterior parts of the body respectively. A equals left anterior and D right posterior, for example.

The direction of combination of movements, primary movement, primary combination, approximate range and direction of technique can be placed on this diagram, as well as the quadrant into which the symptoms fall. Flexion, extension, right lateral flexion and left lateral flexion performed in a single plane are represented by the crossed lines WX and YZ. Rotation is represented by a curved line.

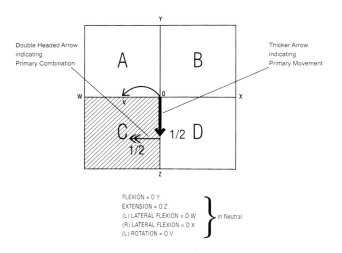

FLEXION = O Y
EXTENSION = O Z
(L) LATERAL FLEXION = O W
(R) LATERAL FLEXION = O X
(L) ROTATION = O V

} In Neutral

Box Diagram 1 Left posterior buttock pain

The primary movement in neutral position is designated by a thicker line and a single headed arrow, the primary combination by a double headed arrow and the range by a vertical or horizontal line which intersects the lines YZ or WX.

This diagram is an attempt to simplify a complicated biomechanical movement. For example, the range of normal flexion performed, say, in left lateral flexion will, of course, be less than the normal range of flexion performed in neutral in a patient without any symptoms. The assessment here is made in relation to movement available on the other side. In Box Diagram 1, the range of extension is considered to be half normal range and left lateral flexion performed in extension is considered to be half the range of right lateral flexion in extension.

There may be times when the symptoms are bilateral or anterior and posterior in distribution, in which case more than one quadrant is hatched and the same principle in relation to movement description is used. Alternatively, more than one diagram may be used for a patient. The quadrant into which symptoms fall is designated by cross hatching.

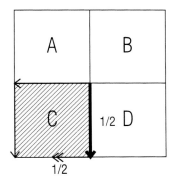

Box Diagram 2: Regular compressive pattern, left posterior buttock pain

In this example, C is the quadrant into which the symptoms fall. Extension is the primary movement but is full range. The symptoms are made worse by extension in left lateral flexion and by left lateral flexion in extension. However, the double headed arrow indicates the primary combination, i.e. left lateral flexion in extension, and the movement is restricted to 1/2 of its normal range (compared to the other side). If extension is the primary movement, then in the examination, extension is performed first before left lateral flexion, and then performed last after left lateral flexion. Assessment is made to decide which combination produces the most severe symptoms. In this case, left lateral flexion in extension is the primary combination and is denoted by a double headed arrow. A similar principle is used for a regular stretch pattern.

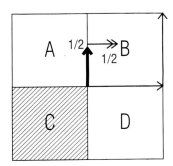

Box Diagram 3: Regular stretch pattern, left posterior buttock pain

In this case, flexion is the primary movement. It is limited to 1/2 normal range and symptoms fall into the C quadrant. The symptoms are made worse with a combination of right lateral flexion in flexion, and flexion in right lateral flexion. However, the primary combination is right lateral flexion in flexion — the double headed arrow. It is limited to 1/2 of its normal range. If rotation is the primary movement, the same principle is often used in the case of the cervical spine; however, a curved arrow is used to indicate the direction of rotation.

Ⓛ Suprascapular Fossa Pain

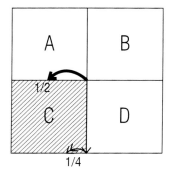

Box Diagram 4: Regular compression pattern, left suprascapular fossa pain
In this diagram, rotation to the left is the primary movement and is restricted to 1/2 range. The symptoms fall into the C quadrant. Left rotation in extension is the primary combination and is restricted to 1/4 range.

Box Diagram 5: Regular stretch pattern, left suprascapular fossa pain
C is the quadrant into which the symptoms fall, and rotation is to the right in primary movement, restricted to 3/4 range. Right rotation in flexion in primary combination is restricted to 1/4 range.

If accessory movements are used, the notation is the same, but with the double arrow direction placed on the outside.

Ⓛ Suprascapular Fossa Pain

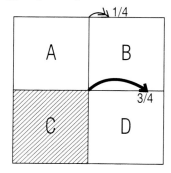

Ⓛ Suprascapular Fossa Pain

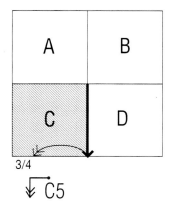

3/4

↓⋅ C5

Box Diagram 6: Regular compression pattern, left suprascapular fossa pain
This diagram indicates that extension is the primary movement, and in full range. Left rotation, limited to 3/4 range in extension, is the primary combination.

When the joint is placed in extension and left rotation, left unilateral pressure on C5 is the most provocative accessory movement.

Patient category

Once the primary movement, primary combination, primary quadrant and accessory movement have been established, the next point to establish is the category of patient. Three categories are recognized and are termed:

a. Acute
b. Subacute
c. Chronic

The choice of category is based upon the responses obtained in the subjective and objective examinations. The aim is to have a simple guide which will establish a starting point in the selection of a direction of movement.

ACUTE category (Movement Diagram 1)
  i. Less than 48 hours onset
  ii. Primary movement is less than 1/2 range
  iii. Pain score is usually greater than 5 on a visual analogue scale (VAS) of 1–10
  iv. May have irregular or regular patterns
  v. On a movement diagram, pain resistance and spasm are present and tend to start before 1/2 range is reached. Usually limited by pain
  vi. Symptoms are usually local, but can be referred.

111

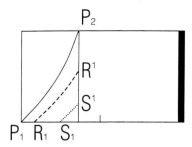

Movement Diagram 1

SUBACUTE category (Movement Diagram 2)
   i. Onset is longer than 48 hours but less than 6 weeks
   ii. Primary movement is equal to, or greater than, 1/2 range
   iii. Pain score is equal to, or less than, 5 on a VAS
   iv. A regular pattern may be dominant, but an irregular pattern can still be present
   v. Movement diagram resistance starts before 1/2 range is reached; pain and spasm are usually present, but are minor. Limited by resistance
   vi. Symptoms may be local or referred.

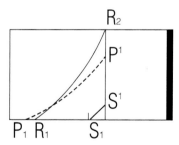

Movement Diagram 2

CHRONIC category (Movement Diagram 3)
   i. Onset is longer than 6 weeks
   ii. Primary movement is greater than 1/2 range
   iii. Pain score is usually less than 5 on a VAS
   iv. Regular patterns usually dominate
   v. Movement diagrams show resistance starting early in the range. Pain graph is low. The limitation is always resistance
   vi. Symptoms are local or referred.

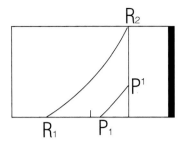

Movement Diagram 3

SELECTION OF INITIAL TREATMENT TECHNIQUE AND PROGRESSION OF TREATMENT

Acute category

In the acute category, with regular stretching or compressive patterns, the direction of the initial procedure is always towards the opposite quadrant and the sequence of techniques is the same as in the testing procedures.

It should be noted, however, that whilst it is logical to apply treatment movement combinations in the same order as examination tests, this may not always be possible, due to certain physical difficulties. If, for example, the treatment movement chosen is passive extension in right lateral flexion, the size of the patient or the stature of the therapist may make this technique very difficult to perform. In this situation, a suitable alternative is to use right side flexion in extension.

A patient presenting with left buttock pain, with a regular compression pattern, could have symptoms represented as shown in Box Diagram 7.

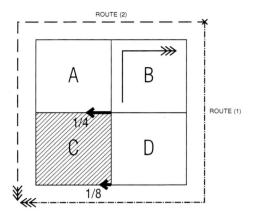

Box Diagram 7
Left lateral flexion is the primary movement, restricted to 1/4 range. Left lateral flexion in extension is the primary combination, restricted to 1/8 range. The first technique chosen is right lateral flexion in flexion, as shown by the 3-headed arrow.

Progression
Route 1

i. (R)	LF	in	F
ii. (R)	LF	in	E
iii. (L)	LF	in	E

or

Route 2

i. (R)	LF	in	F
ii. (L)	LF	in	F
iii. (L)	LF	in	E

Route 1 is probably the less painful direction as it is a more gradual approach to the primary combination of left lateral flexion in extension.

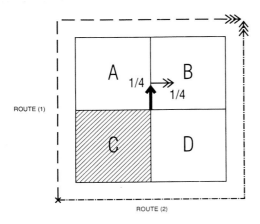

Box Diagram 8
Regular stretch patterns for left buttock pain, acute category, are shown in Box Diagram 8. Flexion is the primary movement, at 1/4 range, and right lateral flexion performed in flexion is the primary combination, also limited to 1/4 range when compared to the range of left lateral flexion in flexion. Symptoms are produced in the C quadrant. The starting position is left lateral flexion in extension.

Suggested sequence
Route 1

i. (L)	LF	in	E
ii. (L)	LF	in	F
iii. (R)	LF	in	F

or

Route 2

i. (L)	LF	in	E
ii. (R)	LF	in	E
iii. (R)	LF	in	F

Route 2 above is likely to be less painful. .

In the categories of subacute and chronic regular stretch and compressive patterns, the same principles can be used. The starting point may be closer to the primary combination, except where distal symptoms and neurological signs are present. In these cases, it is always best to start in the opposite direction and use the same progression as that for an acute category. The following progression may be used, depending on response to treatment.

Subacute category, regular compression pattern

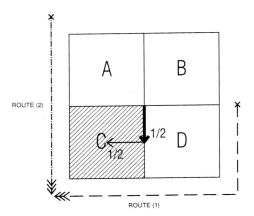

Box Diagram 9

The symptoms fall into the C quadrant. Extension is the primary movement, at 1/2 range, and left lateral flexion in extension in primary combination is restricted to 1/2 range compared to the other side.

Progression

Route 1

i. (R)	LF	in	N
ii. (R)	LF	in	E
iii. (L)	LF	in	E

or

Route 2

i. (L)	LF	in	F
ii. (L)	LF	in	N
iii. (L)	LF	in	E

Route 2 above will probably be the less painful progression, as it is a more gradual approach to the primary movement.

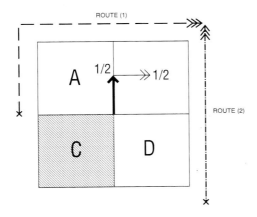

Box Diagram 10

Regular stretch patterns for left buttock pain, subacute category, are shown in Box Diagram 10. Symptoms fall into the C quadrant. Flexion is the primary movement and is at 1/2 range. Right lateral flexion in flexion in primary combination is restricted to 1/2 range compared to the other side.

Suggested sequence

Route 1

i.	(L)	LF	in	N
ii.	(L)	LF	in	F
iii.	(R)	LF	in	F

or

Route 2

i.	(R)	LF	in	E
ii.	(R)	LF	in	N
iii.	(R)	LF	in	F

Route 1 will probably be the less painful progression as it is a more gradual approach to the primary movement.

Chronic category

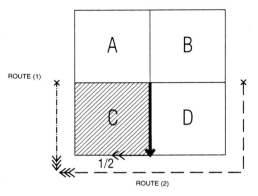

Box Diagram 11

Box Diagram 11 shows the presentation and treatment of a patient with left buttock pain in a regular compression pattern. The primary movement is extension and is full range; the primary combination is left lateral flexion in extension and limited to 1/2 range.

Suggested sequence
Route 1

i.	(L)	LF	in	N
ii.	(L)	LF	in	E

or

Route 2

i.	(R)	LF	in	N
ii.	(R)	LF	in	E
iii.	(L)	LF	in	E

Route 2 is likely to be less painful as it is a more gradual approach to the primary combination.

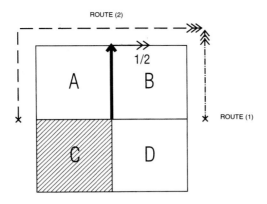

Box Diagram 12
Regular stretch patterns for left buttock pain, chronic category, are shown in Box Diagram 12. Symptoms fall into the C quadrant. Flexion is the primary movement and is full range; right lateral flexion in flexion in primary combination is limited to 1/2 range.

Suggested sequence
Route 1

i.	(R)	LF	in	N
ii.	(R)	LF	in	F

or

Route 2

i.	(L)	LF	in	N
ii.	(L)	LF	in	F
iii.	(R)	LF	in	F

Route 2 will probably be the less painful progression as it is a more gradual approach to the primary combination.

Irregular patterns

It is probably true that, eventually, all patterns will be shown to be regular for some particular anatomical structure or pathological syndrome. However, it is suggested that some irregular patterns may be inflammatory or acutely discogenic in origin. Whatever the case, the same treatment principles described above for regular compressive and stretch patterns can be used.

Box Diagram 13 illustrates acute left buttock pain, irregular pattern.

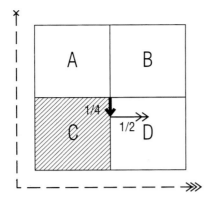

Box Diagram 13
Pain is produced in the C quadrant. Extension is the primary movement and is at 1/4 range. Right lateral flexion in extension is the primary combination and is restricted to 1/2 range compared to the other side. Quadrant A is probably the best starting point because the movement can be directed away from primary combination.

Suggested sequence

i.	(L)	LF	in	F
ii.	(L)	LF	in	N
iii.	(L)	LF	in	E
iv.	(R)	LF	in	E

It is essential to establish some regularity as early as possible and to adjust the technique in relation to this.

ACCESSORY MOVEMENTS

The use of accessory movements in the selection of technique follows the same principles as for physiological movements. Accessory movements can increase or decrease movement that has already occurred at a vertebral segment.

When making the decision as to which accessory technique is selected for use in treatment, two aspects need to be considered:
1. the way in which the direction of the accessory technique may be varied to further increase or decrease the compressive or stretch effect
2. the reproduction of the symptoms by accessory movement.

Cervical spine

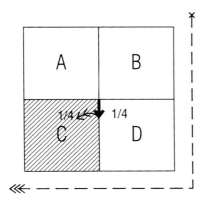

Box Diagram 14

An example of the use of accessory movements in the cervical spine is shown in Box Diagram 14. It represents symptoms from a patient with left suprascapular pain and an acute regular compression pattern. Extension is the primary movement, limited to 1/4 range. Left rotation in extension is the primary combination, and is limited to 1/4 range compared to the other side.

Suggested progression for physiological movement
Route 1

  i. RR   in   F
 ii. RR   in   N
iii. RR   in   E
 iv. LR   in   E

Assuming the level of involvement is c3/4, it can be seen that in RR in F, the left inferior facet of c3 has rotated to the right and moved upwards in relation to the left superior facet of c4. Therefore, postero-anterior pressure over the left inferior facet of c3 will further increase the movement, especially if the pressure is angled cephalad. Postero-anterior pressure over the left superior facet of c4, if angled caudad, will also increase movement, as will antero-posterior pressure when angled caudad. One of these techniques should be chosen as the initial treatment.

In the progression of physiological movements given above, the joint is gradually moved towards a position of LR in E. In this position, the left inferior facet of c3 has rotated to the left and moved down in relation to the left superior facet of c4.

In the position of RR in F, a slight movement towards this end position could be made by an antero-posterior unilateral pressure over the left facet of c3, especially if angled caudad. Postero-anterior pressure over the left superior facet of c4, angled cephalad, will have a similar effect. These movements would produce a slight compression or closing down of the joint on the left hand side. This compressive effect would be further enhanced if the joint was to be placed into RR in N before the application of the accessory technique. The following scheme is the possible progression of the accessory techniques of left unilateral pressure which may be used in the above example.

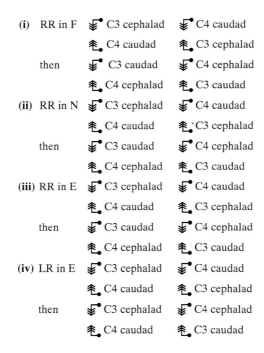

(i) RR in F   C3 cephalad   C4 caudad

              C4 caudad   C3 cephalad

       then   C3 caudad   C4 cephalad

              C4 cephalad   C3 caudad

(ii) RR in N   C3 cephalad   C4 caudad

              C4 caudad   C3 cephalad

       then   C3 caudad   C4 cephalad

              C4 cephalad   C3 caudad

(iii) RR in E   C3 cephalad   C4 caudad

              C4 caudad   C3 cephalad

       then   C3 caudad   C4 cephalad

              C4 cephalad   C3 caudad

(iv) LR in E   C3 cephalad   C4 caudad

              C4 caudad   C3 cephalad

       then   C3 cephalad   C4 cephalad

              C4 caudad   C3 caudad

Symptom Reproduction

Although knowledge of the mechanical effects of the proposed accessory treatment on the joint is useful, it is important to take into account the reproduction of the patient's symptoms. In the above example, if the neutral position — an antero-posterior movement over the left side of c3 — reproduced the shoulder pain of which the patient complained, this technique may be chosen instead of the alternative technique of, e.g. postero-anterior pressure over the left side of c4, if the latter did not reproduce the symptoms as readily as the former. If the patient's problem falls into the category of being severe or irritable, it may be judicious initially to use a technique that does not reproduce the referred pain. In practice, it is often the case that the technique that provokes the symptoms is used, but with the positions of the joints changed such that the pain is no longer reproduced. As progression towards the most painful position is made, it may be that some or all of the patient's symptoms are reproduced during treatment.

Thoracic spine

The same principles apply in the thoracic spine, however the rib articulation needs to be incorporated into the procedures, remembering that unilateral pressure over the angle of the rib has a similar effect on the vertebrae as rotation to the same side, i.e. R3 (angle) produces similar movement to right rotation of T3.

Lumbar spine

The use of accessory movements in the lumbar spine follows similar principles. It is important to realize that unilateral pressure over the facet joints (rather than the transverse processes) is more easily described in terms of the effect on lateral flexion, flexion or extension. For example, consider left buttock pain with an acute regular compressive pattern, as illustrated in Box Diagram 15.

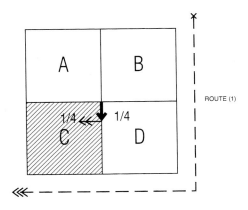

Box Diagram 15
Extension is the primary movement, limited to 1/4 range. Left lateral flexion in extension is the primary combination, limited to 1/4 range compared to the other side. The following progression is adopted.

Route 1

i.	(R)	LF	in	F
ii.	(R)	LF	in	N
iii.	(R)	LF	in	E
iv.	(L)	LF	in	E

The following is the progression of left unilateral pressure.

(i) (R) LF IN F

↘ L3 cephalad

↘ L4 caudad

↘ L3 caudad

↘ L4 cephalad

(ii) (R) LF IN N

↘ L3 cephalad

↘ L4 caudad

↘ L3 caudad

↘ L4 cephalad

(iii) (R) LF IN E

↘ L3 cephalad

↘ L4 caudad

↘ L3 caudad

↘ L4 cephalad

(iv) (L) LF IN E

↘ L4 caudad

↘ L3 cephalad

↘ L4 cephalad

↘ L3 caudad

High cervical spine

Symptoms of mechanical origin here are distributed to the occiput and head. A large proportion of cervical headaches of mechanical causes have their origin in the facet joints and soft tissue of this area.

Accessory movements are the most useful type by far in the high cervical spine. The selection of technique is therefore based on the mechanical principles described in Chapter 4 and the following is the suggested selection and progression of technique.

a) Right sided headache of 0\1 in origin primary combination
F & (R) rotation.

    (i)   C1 in neutral

    (ii)   C1 in F + (R) rotation

    (iii)   C1 in F + (R)

b) (L) sided (H) of 0\1 origin
E + (R) rotation primary combination

    (i)   C1 in neutral

    (ii)   C1 in E + (R) rotation

    (iii)   C1 in E + (R) rotation

c) (R) sided (H) of 1\2 origin
(R) rotation and F primary combination

    (i)   C2 neutral

    (ii)   C1 neutral

    (iii)   C1 (R) rotation and flexion

    (iv)   C2 (R) rotation and flexion

    (v)   C2 (R) rotation and flexion

    (vi)   C1 (R) rotation and flexion

d) (L) sided (H) of 1\2 origin
(L) rotation and extension primary combination

    (i)   C2 neutral

    (ii)   C1 neutral

    (iii)   C1 (L) rotation and extension

    (iv)   Ċ2 (L) rotation and extension

    (v)   C2 (L) rotation and extension

    (vi)   C1 (L) rotation and extension

Selection of technique

SUMMARY OF EFFECTS OF PALPATION

HIGH CERVICAL SPINE	INCREASE JOINT MOVEMENT ON LEFT	DECREASE JOINT MOVEMENT ON LEFT
Examining the left occipital-atlantal complex		
LR in F	↓ C1	↑ C1
RR in E	↑ C1	↓ C1
Examining the left atlanto-axial complex		
F in LR	↑ C1 ↓ C2	↓ C1 ↑ C2
E in LR	↑ C1 ↓ C2	↓ C1 ↑ C2
F in RR	↓ C1 ↑ C2	↑ C1 ↓ C2
E in RR	↓ C1 ↑ C2	↑ C1 ↓ C2

MID CERVICAL Examining left C3-4	INCREASE JOINT MOVEMENT ON LEFT	DECREASE JOINT MOVEMENT ON LEFT
RR in F	C4 C4 caudad	C4 C4 cephalad
	C3 C3 cephalad	C4 C4 caudad
L ROT IN E	C4 C4 cephalad	C4 C4 caudad
	C3 C3 caudad	C3 C3 cephalad
LOW CERVICAL C7-T1 RR in F LR in E	As for C3\4 except clinically on 1st rib increase effect of palpation on left between C6-T1 as above	
THORACIC SPINE T5-6		
LR in E	T5 caudad	T5 cephalad
	T6 cephalad	T6 caudad
	R5	R6
RR in F	T5 cephalad	T5 caudad
	T6 caudad	T6 cephalad
	Rotates T5 to L	R6 Rotates T5 to R
LUMBAR SPINE L3-4		
	L4 cephalad	L3 cephalad
	L3 caudad	L4 caudad
LLF in E	L3 cephalad	L4 cephalad
RLF in F	L4 caudad	L3 caudad

REFERENCES

Grieve G P 1988 Common vertebral joint problems, 2nd edn. Churchill Livingstone, Edinburgh, p 442–447

Maitland G D 1986 Vertebral manipulation, 5th edn. Butterworths, London, p 115–143

Conclusion

There is widespread use of passive movement in the treatment of back pain of mechanical origin. When based on an accurate diagnosis, it provides a useful method of treatment.

Too often various methods claim results which are, at best, unsubstantiated. The fundamentals of accurate history taking, good physical examination, accurate and specific techniques and resultant assessment still provide the basis of sensible treatment.

Practitioners of manipulative therapy have an important part to play in the overall management of back pain; however, their role must be seen in its proper perspective. There is little doubt that those well trained in manipulative therapy can examine the vertebral column competently and administer a technique accurately. Most assess adequately. Combined movements are essentially an adjunct to assist in helping the practitioner of manipulative therapy to improve his skills in the above three aspects.

The application of combined movements should be seen as a simple extension of basic manipulative therapy procedures and practised as such. The more the practitioner uses them, the more skilled he will become.

Deciding on the direction of a technique can be simply approached by using these procedures, but this does not reduce in any way the importance of accurate assessment. It does, however, highlight the importance of the position of the joint rather than the grade of movement as techniques towards the end of the available range are used in the great majority of cases.

Providing that proper examination and assessment are carried out, the categorizing of patients into acute, subacute and chronic categories can help in choosing the direction of technique and the position of the joint for then applying the technique. The progression of the treatment thereafter follows in a straightforward manner.

Performed correctly, combined movements will provide the practitioner with a useful extension to his treatment armamentarium. Their use is always desirable, and occasionally essential, in the management of mechanical back pain by passive movement procedures.

Index